JIM BROWN: The Running Back

The fame of Jim Brown began in 1954 in the Syracuse-Cornell game, when he carried the ball seventeen times for a gain of 151 yards. Later some people would call him the greatest athlete of all time. Others just said he was the greatest runner in football. He did star in many competitive sports, including lacrosse and track, but his great fame was as the running back for the Cleveland Browns. Brown and the Browns were the big story in professional football from 1957 until Jim Brown retired to become an actor.

JIM BROWN:

The Running Back

By Larry Klein

G. P. Putnam's Sons • **New York**

TO JUDY

Ninth Impression

SBN 399-20003-7

© 1965 by Larry Klein

Cop/
J 92
BRO

Published simultaneously in the Dominion of Canada by Longmans Canada Limited, Toronto
Library of Congress Catalog Card Number: 65-20702

PRINTED IN THE UNITED STATES OF AMERICA
10 up

Contents

ACKNOWLEDGMENTS

IN THE last twenty years, Jim Brown's skills have deeply impressed countless people. Many have recorded or remembered what they saw, heard, or felt. The author appreciates their guidance and offers special thanks to the following:

Ed Walsh and Ken Molloy, of Manhasset, who happily helped someone who might help Jim Brown.

Val Pinchbeck, of Syracuse, who cleared conflicting points and opened his office files.

Hal Lebovitz, of Cleveland, who dug deep in his excellent reporting jobs.

Steve Gelman, of New York, who allowed use of *Sport* magazine's photographs and biographical data.

Information was also used from newspaper and magazine clippings contained in the files of the National Football League, the New York *Herald Tribune, Newsweek, Newsday,* and the Syracuse *Herald-Journal.*

It is customary for an author to thank his wife for her patience. Mine is thanked for her patience, proofreading, suggestions, and typing.

Special gratitude is also offered to Jim Brown, whose heroics made this book possible.

L.K.

JIM BROWN: The Running Back

CHAPTER 1

Option 7 and Victory

MAYBE HE was not quite as fast as a speeding bullet or quite as powerful as a locomotive, but Jim Brown certainly looked like Superman early in the fall of 1963.

In the opening game, against Washington, he ran for 162 yards, caught passes for 100 yards, and scored three touchdowns on bursts of 10, 80, and 83 yards.

In the second game, against Dallas, he ran for 232 yards and scored two touchdowns on bursts of 62 and 71 yards.

In the third game, against Los Angeles, he ran for 95 yards and scored his sixth touchdown.

In the fourth game, against Pittsburgh, he ran for 175 yards, scored his seventh touchdown, and frightened Sam Huff's wife.

"My wife phoned me in Washington Saturday night and asked me if I'd seen him in the game on TV," said Huff. "She seemed afraid for me."

Mary Huff and every other National Football League fan knew, of course, that her husband, the linebacker, had to play against fullback Brown the following week. It was no secret, either, that every previous game between Brown's Cleveland Browns and Huff's New York Giants had been a bitter battle. Yet this one threatened to be the most brutal. The Browns, under new coach Blanton Collier, had won their first four games. The Giants had won three of their first four. The Giants, defending champions of the Eastern Conference, were in second place. The Browns were first —but far from overconfident.

Just as a mutual friend had predicted, Jim Brown was polite but firm in rejecting the request for an interview. "No, I'm afraid not," he said over the telephone in his New York hotel room. "We've got a pretty important game tomorrow. I want to concentrate on what I've got to do, then get a good night's sleep. I'll just eat dinner with the team, and we'll all go to a movie."

The movie, ironically, was called *The Running Man.*

"It was lousy," said Brown, and, as things turned out, any resemblance between the movie and the man was purely nonexistent.

October 13, 1963, was a beautiful day for football. Sunny skies, 60-degree temperature, and a light breeze greeted the Sunday afternoon crowd that poured into Yankee Stadium.

But most of the 62,986 fans greeted the visiting Browns somewhat less pleasantly. Light boos accompanied the introductions of the first ten starters. On the eleventh, the public-address announcer never had a chance to be heard. A few cheers only seemed to accentuate the booming boos as No. 32, filling his brown jersey with his muscular upper body and carrying his orange helmet in his left hand, ran between the goal posts and out toward his teammates.

Knowledgeable fans seldom waste their breath on visiting mediocrities. Only the great ones—the Ted Williamses and the Jim Browns—get booed.

If the Giant fans had had any sense that day, they would have used sticks and stones.

With nine minutes gone in the first period, Cleveland losing 7–0 and the ball on the New York 5, Brown bulled his way to the ½-yard line. On the next play, he dived over the middle and scored the tying touchdown.

Early in the third period, with Cleveland losing 17–14 and the ball on the Cleveland 28, Brown exploded. He caught a short screen pass from quarterback Frank Ryan, sidestepped one man, dashed down the left sideline, and, palming the ball in his right hand ("It gives me much better running balance," he said later), simply outran the entire Giant team for the go-ahead touchdown.

Five minutes later, after an exchange of punts and a New York fumble, the Browns moved the Giants' 32. Then Brown did it again. He took Ryan's handoff, charged through left tackle and fought his way to the 25, where he found the lane blocked by heavy player traffic. Swiftly, he swerved to his right and began running parallel to the line of scrimmage. As he ap-

11

proached the right sideline, he picked up a few blockers, turned the corner, and ran the rest of the way into the end zone.

"I usually try to take advantage of whatever my men give me, and today they gave me a lot of good blocking," Brown explained a few minutes after the 35–24 victory. He was standing in front of his gray dressing cubicle, sipping a Pepsi-Cola. He had already taken off his jersey, and the sweat glistened on his heavily muscled chest and arms.

(At rest, half-dressed, Jim Brown looks like what every young man who has ever had sand kicked in his face on the beach would like to look like. His thick neck measures 18 inches, his thin waist 32 inches, and everything in between is a mass of muscle. He is the only back on the team who does not wear hip pads, yet he needs extra holes in his belt to hold up his pants. Below the belt, because "I like to travel light," he wears the smallest-size thigh pads—with the padding cut off—and low-cut, 12½D cleats.)

"What about that second touchdown, the 32-yarder?" asked one of the sportswriters crowded into the steamy dressing room.

Brown considered the question as he considers most questions—without a smile or trace of expression on his ruggedly handsome face. "That's what we call option 7," he said softly. "I have a choice of going anywhere from the center to the outside. I went outside. When you take a chance of cutting against the grain, you're trying to break it all the way. Fortunately, it worked out well when I picked up a few blockers."

"What do you call that pass play where you went 72 yards?" asked another reporter.

"That's just a flare screen," said Brown, beginning to wriggle out of his pants and to reveal his steel-like thighs. "As I was coming down the sideline, I saw [safety man Jim] Patton looking to the inside. He didn't seem to see me. I felt then it was just a matter of sprinting."

When asked if the Browns had used any new plays in their convincing victory, he shook his head. "We had no secret weapons," he said. "And we didn't have to get fancy. We just used our basic stuff and went at them a little more. It's a matter of going out and putting your head into it."

As if to emphasize his words, Brown admitted: "I've got a little headache. It was a very rough ballgame. They were just a little overanxious on a few plays." That was an understatement. The 6-foot-3, 225-pound power package had taken a pounding from the Giant gang-tacklers. His right arm was so swollen he could hardly lift it, and he had reddish welts near both eyes.

After he headed for the showers, in the same slow, rolling shuffle he uses returning to huddles, one of his teammates, halfback Ernie Green, was asked about Brown's performance. "I'm never surprised," said Green. "On every play, I expect him to go all the way. A lot of times when you need it, he'll get it all for you."

In ten years, while Brown played for Syracuse University and later for Cleveland, the New York newspapers had grown accustomed to his pace. But his exploits that day (209 yards gained running and receiving) produced a new torrent of tributes.

"Maybe they should let Jimmy Brown go to work on the Berlin Wall," said the *Mirror*. "He'd smash the thing from end to end just like that."

"It was a little frightening to watch him, let alone to try to catch him," said the *Times*.

"The greatest game ever played by the greatest football player who ever played," said the *Herald Tribune*.

". . . a one-man Cosa Nostra," said the *World-Telegram and Sun*.

"The mighty man from Syracuse," said the *Daily News*, looked like "a steamroller with the maneuverability of a compact car."

The praise was not limited to the press. "There's got to be another league for that guy," Sam Huff said Monday noon. "The way we felt, I didn't think they could score on us yesterday. His two touchdown plays made the difference. He uses his blockers better than ever."

Huff laughed when asked about rumors that Brown was not as good as he used to be. "The only guys I've heard say he's slowing up," said Huff, "are newspapermen or guys on offense, the guys who don't have to play against him."

A few minutes later, Huff, a few of his teammates, and Jim Brown walked into the dining room of Leone's

restaurant, where they were lunch guests of a business-men-fans organization called the Pro Quarterbacks Club. In introducing the men seated at the head table, toastmaster Kyle Rote, a Giant coach, nodded at Brown and dryly remarked, "Jimmy, this is the second day in a row you've had us all for lunch."

Brown gave more than he received. For twenty minutes, with the self-assurance and poise he had perfected in seven years as a professional, he spoke and answered questions about himself, his team, his new coach, Blanton Collier, and his old coach, Paul Brown.

"This is the first time we've come to New York without thinking of internal problems," Jim admitted. "We have a new attitude in Cleveland. We feel we have a coach who will listen to ideas and share ideas with us. I think Paul Brown was a tremendous coach, but Blanton has a little more compassion for people."

Many in his audience knew that thoughtful, sensitive Jim Brown was probably the player most responsible for getting coach Brown fired the previous January. Paul had been the first and only coach of the team named after him, and from 1946 through 1957 he had been the most successful coach in pro-football history. In those 12 seasons, his Browns won 11 division championships. But from 1958 on, as the NFL grew more balanced, the Browns won no titles and the players lost respect for coach Brown's aloof, ironhanded, I'll-do-all-the-thinking-and-play-calling system. Whenever a player grumbled, he was either traded or treated as a chronic complainer. But soon after Jim Brown publicly announced that "it's no good to play under a feeling of tension, of suppression of the individual," Paul Brown was replaced by his longtime assistant, Blanton Collier.

As he looked around Leone's, Jim seemed to sense what was on many minds. "There is no animosity against Paul at all," he said. "I sort of feel sorry for him. He is a great coach and a great man, with a lot of pride. There were just a couple of adjustments he could have made. It was such a tragedy that he didn't."

Yet from the way Jim talked during the question-and-answer period neither he nor his teammates missed Paul Brown during their first five victories. "I used to be the silent one," he admitted. "Now I give suggestions and try to do everything I can to help. All of our players now try to help the other guy. Blanton will call some of the plays, Ryan will call some, [spotter-coach] Dub Jones will send some down, and even I call some once in a while.

"It becomes ridiculous," he continued, "when you've got a minute to go and you need as many plays as you can get, and you have to sit down and wait for the messenger guards to come in. Now the other teams can't get ready while we wait for a play from the bench."

When Jim finished speaking, the hearty applause left no doubts that his plain sincerity was appreciated as much as his playing skill. Before he left the restaurant and headed back to Cleveland, he shook many hands and heard many words of praise. Yet the most meaningful came from the man whose NFL rushing records Brown broke. "Christ," said former Philadelphia star Steve Van Buren, shaking hands, "you've gained more yardage in one game than I used to in five."

It was the type of tribute that twenty-seven-year-old Jim Brown had been earning since boyhood.

CHAPTER 2

Young Man of Manhasset

THE earliest years of Jim Brown's life have been, to say the least, a source of conflicting testimony.

Depending on what national publication you had read, and when, you could have learned that Jim's first home was in (1) a slum in Manhasset, New York, (2) a Negro cabin in Georgia, or (3) a four-bedroom house in Georgia.

You also could have learned that he was raised by his (1) grandmother, (2) great-grandmother, or (3) great-great-grandmother until he was (1) six or (2) seven years old.

The answers to this multiple-choice test are that James Nathaniel Brown was born February 17, 1936, on St. Simon's Island, Georgia, and raised there in a four-bedroom home by his great-grandmother until he was nearly nine years old.

At that point, his mother sent for him and he moved

north to Manhasset, Long Island, where his mother worked as a domestic in the homes of wealthy people.

In Manhasset, he began playing organized sports.

Jim was only in the seventh grade at Manhasset's Plandome Road School when he first attracted attention in athletics. And that was somewhat of an accident, according to veteran Manhasset High football coach Edward Walsh. One hot day a while ago, gray-haired Walsh explained it this way:

"Coaches in the school system said, 'We have two young boys who are the best athletes ever to have gone through here.' So I went to practice and watched an intramural football game near the end of the season and an intramural basketball game at the start of that season. Later, one coach came to me and asked, 'What did you think of those two boys?'

" 'Frankly, I can't tell you,' I said. 'I was so busy watching another boy named Jimmy Brown.' I was kidding. I had seen the two boys, but had paid more attention to Jimmy. He had such great moves and he was so relaxed."

Walsh's face suddenly spread into a wide grin, and his eyes actually twinkled. Obviously, his mind had flashed back to the first time he ever saw young Brown. "He was a pudgy, short little boy," said Walsh, smiling. He savored each descriptive word. "That relaxed on that level. Every ounce of energy was used for a purpose."

By the time Jim reached the ninth grade, many Manhasset sports fans could hardly wait to see him in action. Even the superintendent of schools suggested, quite politely, that it might be a good idea to jump Jim right onto the varsity.

Coach Walsh disagreed. "It was a policy I had," he recalled, "to let boys play with their junior-high teams and let them develop a winning complex." Brown did. He and his teammates on the Manhasset freshman football squad marched through the season undefeated, untied, and unscored upon.

Before the beginning of Brown's sophomore season, coach Walsh, as always, explained his system to the squad. He said, in effect, that each boy would be graded on his performances in scrimmages and games and that the boy with the highest grade at each position would start the next game. "And if you have any complaints," Walsh wound up, "instead of going downtown and telling your friends, come in to me and we'll talk it over."

After the opening game, a 33–0 victory in which he scored one touchdown but played less than a half, halfback Brown did go in and talk it over. As Walsh remembers, he repeated the grading system. Jim realized for the first time how it operated and, without another incident, "he worked for that grade the rest of his school career."

Jim's results ranged from the remarkable to the phenomenal.

In his sophomore season, while the team won six of its seven games, he set a school record by averaging 7.4 yards a carry.

In his junior season, while the team again won six of its seven games, he scored 14 touchdowns and averaged a staggering 15.1 yards a carry.

In his senior season, while the team won all of its seven games, he scored 20 touchdowns (and 12 extra points), won an award as Nassau County's most outstanding player, and earned high school All-American honors. But his average dropped to 14.9 yards a carry.

In his defense, though, it should be noted that his total playing time for the powerful Indians that season equaled only about four full games. And opponents stacked their defenses against the 6-foot-1, 193-pound threat. When he went in motion, the other team's best defensive man matched him step for step. When he started to swing around left end on his favorite play, L-57 (a very quick pitchout from the quarterback), two or three men were usually there already, trying to cut off his route.

When all else failed, some opponents tried to get Jim angry enough to fight and get thrown out of the game. "I used to hear what was being yelled—bad things, racial things and anything," said Walsh. "But he never lost his head. I'd call him to the sideline and he'd always tell me, 'Don't worry, Mr. Walsh, don't worry. I won't get angry.' "

Jim rarely expressed any emotion, even to those who helped him on and off the field. "You could never tell what he was thinking," said Walsh, who has been one of Jim's strongest admirers for seventeen years. "You had to work and work to find out what was bothering him. He was too quiet. He wasn't one to go out and ask people to help him solve his problems. He'd go off alone and ponder his problems and think these things through. He had a lot of wisdom for a boy his age."

An only child, whose parents worked and sometimes lived apart in Manhasset, Jim spent a great deal of off-field time by himself. His clothes were very neat, but he had very little money.

"One time, near the end of his junior year, he was out of school for five days," recalled Walsh. "When I found out he wasn't ill, I got in the car and started to hunt for him. I finally found him and remember putting him into the car and driving to Fordham to watch spring football practice. I hoped that would help loosen him up. He told me he was contemplating joining the service and not finishing high school. When I finally got from him what his actual problem was—he just didn't have any food. As I recall, he had had only one piece of cake in five days.

"I don't remember his exact words, but they were something like: 'Mr. Walsh, you just don't know what it feels like to go through school and get through practice with no food.' "

Though he seldom started conversations, Jim startled Walsh with his maturity. Jim was a sophomore, but only fourteen years old, when Walsh asked him one day what he wanted out of life.

"It'll have to be sports," said Jim.

As Walsh recalled, Jim's reasoning was that "anything he tried in life seemed to follow a pattern. He would start to have success, which spurred him on to improve. Then eventually there was the heartache of color. The only exception to that was sports. So he decided it would have to be sports."

Despite his natural athletic ability, Jim might never be known outside Long Island today if it had not been for his burning desire to excel. "That's the key thing, the part people don't realize—how much work he put into developing these skills," said Walsh. "That desire caused him to work hour after hour. A month at a time, I've seen him eat a quick lunch, run out on the field, and work alone for the rest of the hour. If he wanted to learn something, he'd work during lunch hour, after school in regular practice, and again in the evening. I'd get a call from his mother at night, asking if there was any way I could get him to go in the house and do his homework."

His desires and skills, of course, extended far beyond the football field.

In track, he was an all-round performer who set a school record with a high jump of 6 feet 3.

In lacrosse, he was all-scholastic as a sophomore. As a junior, he was so impressive that a college coach near the end of the season said, "That fellow is probably as good as any college player I've seen this season." But he did not play his senior season. Instead, he switched to baseball, because the New York Yankees sent a letter inviting him to try out.

In baseball, he made the team as a pitcher and a first-baseman. As a batter, he hit the ball about as far

as anybody in school—when he connected. But he never considered himself good enough to go try out.

In basketball, he was all-scholastic and led the county in scoring as a junior. As a senior, he averaged 38 points a game. That figure might have been considerably higher if he had played for a stronger team. In the opening game, he set a Long Island scoring record with 23 field goals and seven foul conversions for 53 points. But his team lost, 93–69. His record lasted five days—until he broke it in the second game, with 55 points. His team won that game, 94–60, but for most of the remaining games Jim, instead of leading the fast break, as he had done earlier, was used to bring the ball upcourt.

"The typical pattern," said Walsh, who also coached basketball at that time, "was that he'd feed somebody, they'd shoot and miss, and he'd follow up and put it in.

"Though at 6-1 he was not tall as basketball players go, he was jumping center and was never outjumped that I can recall. He was tremendous on the boards. He had excellent hands and a tremendous amount of spring in his legs, and he could hang there in the air. He could do about anything."

As a tribute to his sports accomplishments (thirteen letters in five sports), Jim's fellow students at Manhasset High voted to retire his football jersey, No. 33. It was the first time in the school's history that an athlete had been so honored. But instead of the big-to-do that usually accompanies such a ceremony, Coach Walsh simply locked Jim's jersey in a metal cabinet, where it remains today. "When he quits showing people what he can do as a professional, then I think we should bring it out and frame it," explains Walsh. "Then we can have the memories and say this was Jim Brown, but what's the sense now? Week after week, he's still proving how great he is."

Outside sports, Jim was somewhat less successful. He was chief justice of the school court, but below average in some of his classwork. Still, at one time or another, about forty-five colleges and universities expressed interest in recruiting him.

He ended up at Syracuse, as most people know yet the frightening fact is that he almost did not go to any major school at all.

The day after Labor Day, 1956, only two or three weeks before freshmen everywhere had to report to college, a Manhasset lawyer named Ken Molloy bumped into a high school official and asked where young Brown was going to college. When told probably a small Negro school in North Carolina, Molloy —an avid sports fan and former lacrosse star at Syracuse (class of '42)—became infuriated. He asked a mutual friend to bring Jim to his home that night.

After Jim arrived, Molloy asked him if he would be interested in going to Syracuse if he could get in. Jim said yes, and Molloy said he'd see what he could do. He quickly called Arnie Burdick, a friend from Syracuse and at that time the university's sports publicity director. The two arranged for Jim to fly to Syracuse on the first plane out of New York the next morning.

Before he hung up, Burdick asked how he would recognize Brown at the airport. Molloy said, "Don't worry, you'll recognize him."

Molloy was obviously right, for four years later Burdick, by then a Syracuse sportswriter, reminiscingly wrote: "A young giant skipped off the ship, and his every movement was a picture of smoothness and grace and coordination.

"The muscleman introduced himself, but not even then was this necessary, for he towered over everyone in the airport, and his broad, huge shoulders barely squeezed through doorways. When he hopped into the car, we naturally listed to his side, for he was 205 pounds then, and his quietness—almost shyness—and politeness were becoming to a seventeen-year-old."

Jim's looks also impressed the coaches he met that day. His marks in the entrance examinations, however, were something else. Syracuse soon advised Molloy that Jim had not done well enough to be accepted. More determined than ever that a Syracuse acceptance would be a "damn good thing for Jim and the school, and I wasn't going to let a poor judgment frustrate this kid," Molloy met the challenge head on. He went to Dr. Raymond Collins, superintendent of schools in Manhasset and an experienced educator who had followed Jim's academic career closely for years, and obtained assurance that Jim could do the work if accepted. Next, Molloy called a friend who called a friend who pulled the string that put Jim Brown into Syracuse University.

"Jimmy was pretty sure he could do the job athletically," Molloy recalled in his Manhasset law office one day a while ago. "He recognized he hadn't done the job academically that he could have at Manhasset, but he had confidence he could do it at Syracuse."

Not so certain athletically or academically, Syracuse said it had given out its full allotment of freshman scholarships, and that it could provide no financial assistance for Jim's first semester. If any scholarship money became available in the second semester, the school said, it would go to Jim, but at least until then he would have to pay his own way.

Naturally, that kind of money—about a thousand dollars—was well beyond what Jim or his family could provide. But having come that far, Molloy was doubly determined. He sent Brown to Syracuse in September and began raising the money in October.

CHAPTER 3

Syracuse: The Start

"DEAR MR.————," began the form letter, and Ken Molloy made sure it was received by the right people in town.

You were undoubtedly one of those who felt pretty proud of Jimmy Brown and his athletic record at Manhasset High School. When he finished last June, he was probably Nassau County's outstanding athlete of all time.

There was good reason for our pride in this fine young American—and there will be more. But we need your help. That is, Jimmy Brown needs it. Here is the situation:

Jimmy recently matriculated at Syracuse University. When he did this, he relied upon the assurance of certain residents of Manhasset that they would contribute toward his expenses there. Frankly, Jimmy and his family cannot handle that, for it will come to about $1,000 for this semester.

Given this chance, however, Jimmy will, we are convinced, give us in Manhasset ample reason to continue our confidence in him as an athlete and as a representative of all that is fine in young American manhood.

Several of us have joined to see what can be done to give Jimmy Brown his big chance. We think it will be one of Manhasset's soundest investments.

We think, too, that you may feel the same way about this or you would not have gotten this letter. If you agree, please send us your check . . .

Donations of from five to a hundred dollars each came in from about forty-five people, Molloy made up the difference, and Brown's first semester was taken care of. (Since school aid did not come the second semester either, Molloy engineered another drive that paid the way.)

If it had been a Hollywood movie, the rest of the reel might have featured scenes where halfback Brown broke loose in a practice scrimmage, zigzagged through the entire team while his coach stared in wide-eyed disbelief, won a starting position, and starred throughout the freshman season.

But it was real life. More specifically, it was Syracuse, which was then slightly wary of Negro athletes because of a few troublesome incidents in the past.

Jim did start and did play a reasonable amount of time in the freshman opener against the Army plebes. Ken Molloy attended the game and sat near some top-ranking officers. "All they did at the beginning," he recalled, "was to complain about the poor Army tackling when Jimmy carried the ball. But by the end, they were saying how good he was. I kept personal statistics. Jimmy averaged more than eight yards every time he carried the ball. I came home very relieved."

If the Syracuse coaches were extremely excited about Brown's performance, they certainly did not show it. They gave everyone a chance to play and did not start him again until the final game of the short season. Colgate crushed Syracuse that day, but "Jimmy showed such great class even in losing," said Molloy, who readily admitted he was rather prejudiced.

After the game, Molloy visited the room young Brown was living in near the campus. As Molloy recalled, "I found a bunch of comic books there and threw them in the wastebasket and raised heck with him."

Molloy continued to stress academics to Jim. A week after the seventeen-year-old freshman wrote him a letter, Molley answered it in this way: "I return herewith your letter of November 18th with indications in the margin of seven rather obvious errors you have made in either spelling or grammatical construction. I would suggest you review same and I am sure it will help your English."

Molloy turned out to be more a prophet than a proofreader. He ended the same letter with: "Jim, after talking to your coaches, I have not changed my opinion that you will be one of the greatest athletes of all time at Syracuse University. You are the only one who can deny yourself from reaching to great heights. So, keep a proper attitude. . . ."

His entire first year at Syracuse, especially after not playing that much in freshman basketball though scoring well, was a depressing experience for Jim.

"I was sorry about being there," he said years later. "I felt that I always was being shunted aside. I didn't seem to be wanted."

"Jimmy would call me, and I could tell right away he was miserable," his high school girl friend, Henrietta Creech, once told New York sportswriter Milton Gross. "He'd tell me he was going to quit, and I'd want to know why. 'I'm getting shoved around,' he'd say. 'Nothing I do seems to satisfy the coaches. Any time a play goes wrong you'd think it was my fault.' "

Jim also called Molloy occasionally, and by the end of that freshman year, Molloy remembered, "the discontent had set in. That summer he came into the office—I'm sure he did a lot of soul-searching—and said he didn't feel he could be happy at Syracuse, that it might be better for all concerned to move on."

Immediately Molloy called a friendly coach at Syracuse. The conversation, according to Molloy, went:

"Jim feels he's had it at Syracuse and doesn't feel he's being recognized," said Molloy.

"Jim has great justification for this feeling," said the coach. "However, I feel I know [varsity football coach] Ben Schwartzwalder. If he felt he could win playing his grandmother, he'd play his grandmother. I'm sure

Jim will get a chance. If he's the better man at his position, he'll play."

The two men hung up, and when Jim heard the coach's reassuring words that he would get a chance, recalled Molloy, "That was it. It dissipated his feeling. That's all he wanted."

Next, in a casual conversation that seemed right out of a Grade B Jim Thorpe movie, Molloy suggested that Brown enter the national decathlon competition scheduled for Atlantic City, New Jersey, early in the summer. Jim agreed, and his training for the grueling, two-day, ten-event competition was as casual as the conversation about entering it. For a week or so he worked out on Manhasset High's field—running, jumping, and throwing. The shotput and discus were the most difficult to practice, because the weights were so heavy that Molloy and Jim's other friends had to roll them back.

Then Jim went to Atlantic City and, competing in a few events for the first time, finished 10th against 22 of the nation's top decathlon men. He scored 5,029 points; Bob Richards, the twenty-eight-year-old track star who won the 1952 Olympic pole vault, won with 6,501 points. Jim's best events were the discus, where he finished fourth (132 feet, 8 inches) and the high jump, where he tied for fourth (5 feet, 9¾ inches). Naturally, he had competed in both before. And, naturally, the events he had never competed in were the ones he did poorest in. He lost many points by finishing in a 14th-place tie in the pole vault (10 feet), 18th in the

400-meter run (56.3 seconds) and 20th in the 110-meter high hurdles.

"If Brown had concentrated on track and stayed around 200–205 pounds, he would have made the Olympic decathlon team in 1956," Syracuse track coach Bob Grieve once said. He was probably right, judging from Jim's improvement in one year.

In the 1955 decathlon, he finished fifth. Bob Richards won again, with 6,873 points, but Jim jumped his point total 550 to 5,579.

If any one year in Jim Brown's brilliant athletic career can be considered a crucial turning point, it must be that sophomore year at Syracuse.

He lettered in basketball and scored 14.9 points a game, the second highest total on the team.

He lettered in track and scored 28 points in one meet against Alfred University.

He lettered in lacrosse and sometimes frightened opposing goalies. "He was fantastic," recalls Dick Schaap, a columnist for the New York *Herald Tribune*, who was a senior at Cornell when Brown was a sophomore at Syracuse. "We triple-manned him whenever he had the ball, which is something like putting four men on Wilt Chamberlain. Still he'd duck, weave, push men out of his way, and come in to shoot. In the one game I played against him, he took seven shots and scored four goals. The other three shots bounced off me so fast I never saw them."

But most important, that year Brown proved he could star in football if given the chance.

CHAPTER 4

Syracuse: The Stardom

IT IS only one decade, but it seems like thousands of light-years ago.

Today, when all the great runners in all professional football history are listed—Jim Thorpe, Bronko Nagurski, Ernie Nevers, Red Grange, and others ad infinitum—Jim Brown almost always tops the list.

In 1954, when only the runners at one position in one college in one state were listed, the situation was startlingly, incredibly, different.

The left halfbacks at Syracuse, according to the team's depth chart prepared before Brown's sophomore season began, ranked from top to bottom in this order:

Sam Alexander
Lyle Carlson
Ed Ackley
Bill Micho
Dick Jackson
Jim Brown

Though none of the first five could be described as an All-American threat, each had a better chance of playing than Brown did at first. By mid-season, however, Jim had worked his way up far enough to be called on to carry 13 times against powerful Illinois. Syracuse lost, 34–6, but Brown averaged 5 yards a carry and strengthened his standing as a substitute who could produce.

Two weeks later, with Syracuse carrying a mediocre record of two victories and three defeats, Jim was given a true test. Early in the game against Cornell, when regular right halfback Art Troilo was injured, left halfback Ray Perkins replaced him and Brown replaced Perkins. Syracuse lost the game but gained a star.

In the second period, with Cornell leading 7–0, Brown sprinted 30 yards on one play and 25 on another, helping move the ball to the Cornell 17-yard line. Syracuse surged to a first down on the 7 only to be pushed back to the 22 by a penalty. Then Brown carried four times and bulled back to the 2, but it was not enough and Cornell took over on downs.

In the fourth period, with Cornell leading 14–0, Brown did it all at once. He took a pitchout on his own 46-yard line, headed wide around right end, stumbled almost out of bounds when hit, regained his balance, faked one tackler out of the way, sidestepped two others, and ran the rest of the way to the end zone. The 54-yard touchdown ended the day's scoring.

In all that afternoon, Brown carried 17 times and gained 151 yards and a starting position.

"I guess you'd have to say this was the turning point in my career," he said years later. "Up until that time, I had been just another player on a pretty good team. But from that Cornell game on, I was first string."

He solidified his starting position the very next week at Archbold Stadium in full view of 37,000 fans, who accounted for the highest gate receipts in Syracuse football history.

On the sixth play of the game, against previously undefeated but twice-tied Colgate, a bitter upstate New York rival, Ray Perkins dashed 23 yards for a touchdown. Minutes later, Brown dashed 17 yards for a touchdown. Colgate took longer but finally tied the score, 12–12, going into the final period.

Then it was Syracuse's turn—or, more specifically, Brown's turn. Starting from his own 23, he carried on five of six plays and almost singlehandedly moved the ball to the Colgate 41. On the next play, he got the ball again, swept around right end, and sprinted down the sideline all the way to the tie-breaking touchdown. That was the stroke that cut Colgate's resistance, and Syracuse rolled on to a 31–12 upset.

A sportswriter in the dressing room afterward asked Brown if that had been his greatest day in football. "You mean high school, too, sir?" asked Jim.

"Yes."

"I probably had better days in high school," Jim said, "but I never had a better feeling than I do now. This game really gets a guy."

Still polite, still honest, yet somehow changed. Jim

40

Brown was beginning to like Syracuse. And, of course, Syracuse was liking Jim Brown more and more.

The mutual-admiration society intensified its feeling during the football season of 1955.

After an uneventful opening loss to Pittsburgh, junior Jim Brown began rolling the bandwagon. It picked up jumpers-on a few at a time at first and dozens at a time by the end of the season.

Against Boston University, in a Saturday night game, Brown led Syracuse to a 27–12 victory by scoring on runs of 24 and 66 yards and kicking three extra-point conversions in three attempts. A third touchdown run, also of 24 yards, was nullified by an illegal-use-of-hands penalty.

After the game, *The New York Times* identified Jim as "one of the most dangerous backs in the East."

Against Army the following week, Syracuse put together a powerful team effort and defeated the three-touchdown favorite, 13–0. It was one of the most shocking upsets in the country, and one of the biggest reasons for it was Brown. Though he scored only one point, he helped control the ball in the steady rain at Michie Stadium. He carried 17 times for 67 of Syracuse's 110 yards rushing. The entire Army team gained 78 yards on the ground.

After that game, *The New York Times* went even further, calling Jim "one of the best backs of the year."

The usually reserved *Times* said it first, but countless newspapers, players, coaches, officials, and fans were soon to follow.

If Syracuse had any illusions of grandeur after upsetting Army, Maryland swiftly deflated them. The Terrapins gave a pointed demonstration of why they were ranked second in the nation and how they had won ten consecutive games since 1954. They scored the first time they got the ball, stretched their lead to 20–7 at halftime, and scored twice more in the first seven minutes of the third period. They also forced Brown to fumble and lose the ball the second time he carried, but after the 34–13 victory they paid high praise to the halfback who had gained 74 yards and a touchdown against their rugged defense.

"If Brown were playing behind our line, he would run right out of the stadium," said senior center Bob Pellegrini. "That kid really played some ballgame for Syracuse."

Sports columnist Jack Slattery of the Syracuse *Herald-Journal* noted: "For two weeks in a row, Brown has been outstanding against a first-rate line. From here on in, he should be something special to watch."

The momentum was building.

Holy Cross was next. A Homecoming crowd of 24,000 in Worcester, Massachusetts watched the mismatch. Syracuse won, 49–9. Jim scored only three points, but he thrilled the crowd with his running (45 yards), receiving (41 yards), and kick returning (157 yards)—and tired out at least one game official.

On one Holy Cross punt, Jim caught the ball on his own 26, faked a handoff, headed to the right sideline, found his way blocked, reversed his field, raced almost all the way to the left sideline, and finally fell to a tackler after running more than 100 yards and gaining 56. As umpire Len Dobbins reached down to take the ball away, he supposedly said, "Take it easy on us officials, Jim. Run straight for a change. We're getting exhausted."

The following week's score was Penn State 21, Jim Brown 20. The Manhasset mauler scored all his team's points and would have tied Penn State if one of his conversion kicks hadn't been blocked. For State, star quarterback Milt Plum plunged for one touchdown, passed for one, and kicked all three conversions; star halfback Lenny Moore ran for one touchdown and 145 yards. For Syracuse, Brown carried 20 times, gained 155 yards, kicked two conversions, and scored three touchdowns. The performance pleased a key man.

"I would say that Saturday Jimmy played the best ball for us in his career here," said Syracuse coach Ben Schwartzwalder. "He played well both on offense and defense. And in the last two games Jim has shown marked improvement. He's starting to figure things out, and he's come to the point where he's fully aware there's a lot more to this game than just grabbing that ball and running with it."

The bandwagon rolled on.

The traditional game against Colgate at Archbold Stadium drew a record crowd of 39,500, including Governor Averell Harriman. Of the 82 yards Jim gained, the final 4—with less than three minutes remaining—were the most important. They represented the game-winning touchdown. Syracuse won, 26–19.

Jim had starred in the heat, in the cold, and in the rain, and in the season finale he starred in the snow.

Against West Virginia, a one-touchdown favorite, he faced a rugged defensive star named Sam Huff, who was then a senior. Though warned by his coaches to keep the ball away from Brown, Huff booted the opening kickoff right at him. Brown caught the ball on the 10 and quickly brought the crowd to its feet. He raced 71 yards—all the way to the West Virginia 19—before he was stopped. On the second play from scrimmage, from the 16, he swept around right end and sprinted to a touchdown—only to have it nullified by a penalty.

Jim's only scoring after that was two extra points, but he had showed his teammates it could be done. Syracuse won, 20–13.

In the course of the upset, Brown and Huff collided more than a few times. Brown averaged 4 yards for 21 carries; all Huff gained were two broken teeth and a cut between the eyes that is still a scar today. Their rivalry was to continue, of course. But first Brown had to play his final—and best—season of college football.

CHAPTER 5

All-Everything

IN LATE August 1956, Jim Brown came down with a case of mumps and was forced to miss the first few days of pre-season football practice. It was just about the only time in his entire senior year that anything or anybody stopped him.

Jim joined the Syracuse squad on September 7, and some ten days later the university's new sports publicity director, Val Pinchbeck, had to go to Maryland to talk up his team for the opening game. "I was down there a week, saying Jim Brown was a great football player," Pinchbeck recalled years later. "Of course, I really had no idea since I had never seen him play except for one game as a sophomore. And coach Tommy Mont's boys were cocky. They hadn't lost in fifteen regular-season games."

The University of Maryland—and Val Pinchbeck—were startled by what they saw the Saturday afternoon of September 22. "When that kickoff came, splat! He ran right through them," said Pinchbeck.

Brown plunged 4 yards for one touchdown, scored a second touchdown on a 24-yard pass play, and set up a third touchdown on a 78-yard run. Over-all, in 18 carries, he rushed for 154 yards. The entire Maryland team rushed for 153 yards and lost, 26–12.

That night, as he was driving back to Syracuse, Pinchbeck heard a radio announcer praising the play of "scatback" Jim Brown. "I've never forgotten that," said Pinchbeck, "and I've always wondered what that guy's reaction would have been if our 212-pound 'scatback' had wandered into his studio."

Many more people learned—and talked—about Brown in the following weeks after Syracuse lost to powerful Pittsburgh.

Against West Virginia, he carried 22 times, gained 165 yards, scored two touchdowns, and kicked three extra points in the 27–20 victory. "He's a marvel," said losing coach Art Lewis.

Against Army, he carried 22 times again, gained 125 yards, set up the game's only touchdown with a 36-yard run, kicked the extra point, and saved the victory with his defensive strength.

Though never known as a defensive demon, Brown was that day, in front of 40,051 fans (the largest crowd ever to attend a college game in upstate New York) and a regional television audience. Once, Army halfback Gil Roesler turned his left end, broke into the open, and seemed headed for the tying touchdown. But

Brown caught him from behind. Another time, late in the last period, the Cadets threatened again. They had the ball on the Syracuse 7, first down and goal to go. They ended up 1 yard short four plunges later. Three of the tackles, single-handedly or in tandem, were made by Brown.

He needed little help against Boston University. He scored every Syracuse point in the 21–7 victory. "The greatest back I've seen since Glenn Davis," said losing coach Buff Donelli.

To the football fans of the mid-1940's, Glenn Davis was what Red Grange had been in the mid-1920's— the most exciting college runner around. His speed and broken-field ability carried halfback Davis onto the All-American team three times and helped Army march through three seasons undefeated. But unlike Grange, Davis did not do it all alone. He had a powerful partner named Doc Blanchard, a three-time All-American fullback who specialized in blasting through the middle of opposing lines when Davis was not dashing around the ends. They were known as Mr. Inside and Mr. Outside, and were discussed separately about as rarely as Abbott without Costello or corned beef without cabbage. Yet as individuals, both Blanchard and Davis were specialists. Each ran brilliantly—but in only one direction.

One week after BU coach Buff Donelli called Jim Brown the greatest since Davis, Penn State coach Rip Engle studied Jim Brown in action and called him "the most powerful runner since Doc Blanchard."

47

That period also produced one of the very few legends about Brown of Syracuse.

A seventh-grade teacher in Syracuse, so the story goes, asked her class to write an essay on the man they admired most. One third of the students wrote about President Eisenhower; two thirds wrote about Jim Brown. "You would think," one youngster supposedly wrote, "that the University would be smart enough to give him another three-year contract."

Alas, those essays written for Miss Sonia Dalrymple's English class at the Lincoln School were never published in full. Yet the story about them in the Syracuse *Herald-Journal* of November 11, 1956, made no mention of "two thirds." Nor did any of the five letters quoted mention "another three-year contract."

Heading into its final game of the season against Colgate, Syracuse faced three solid incentives.

If the team won, it would establish the school's best football record (7–1) since 1923.

If the team won convincingly, it would earn a New Year's Day bowl bid.

If Jim Brown gained 17 yards rushing, he would break the school's season record of 805 yards, set by George Davis in nine games in 1949.

Colgate had as much chance that day as General Custer had at Little Big Horn.

When the massacre ended, Syracuse had:

Won, 61–7.

Clinched a Cotton Bowl bid.

And Jim Brown had:

Gained 197 yards in 22 carries (a Syracuse school record for rushing).

Scored 43 points (a national collegiate record for scoring) by kicking seven points after and collecting touchdowns on respective runs of 1, 15, 50, 8, 19, and 1 yards.

Convinced the crowd of 39,701 (a sellout) that his best run was one that didn't count. Early in the third period, after he had scored all his team's 27 points in the first half, he started around end and looked trapped 10 yards behind the line of scrimmage. Somehow, he shook loose from three or four tacklers and stumbled down the sideline for another touchdown. But the play was nullified by a clipping penalty.

No one knew it at the time, but Brown had broken the major-college scoring record by one point. He would have missed it if Syracuse had had a reasonably accurate place-kicker to replace him. After an early touchdown, a left-footed substitute came in and kicked a conversion attempt shockingly far off target. This so disgusted coach Schwartzwalder that even when he had his first team on the bench, he sent in Brown to kick the extra points.

The final-game spree catapulted Brown up to 106 points (a season record at Syracuse) and into third place (behind two ten-game players) in the national rushing race. He gained 986 yards in 158 carries, a startling 6.2-yard average. This also made him an All-American and a marked man in the Cotton Bowl against Texas Christian University.

Yet his phenomenal success on the football field did little to change Jim off the field. Always the strong, silent type (by nature, not because he felt he was better than the others), he spoke little to his teammates and less to his coaches.

"Going to that Cotton Bowl game," coach Schwartzwalder once told sportswriter Bill Heinz, "we worked at Norman, Oklahoma, and I could tell something was bothering Jim. I asked him, and he said, 'Well, I need a haircut. The hair on the back of my neck rubs on my jersey and I can't run.'

"Now, getting him a haircut in Oklahoma wasn't as easy as it is in Syracuse. Finally, one of our coaches found a Negro taxi driver and he took Jim to a barber shop. When they found out who he was, they made a big fuss over him and somebody made him lunch. That relaxed Jim . . ."

And almost ruined TCU. On New Year's Day in Dallas, before a crowd of 68,000 and a national television audience, Brown played 56 minutes and did nearly everything for Syracuse but clean cleats. He kicked off, completed a pass for 20 yards, returned three kickoffs for 96 yards, carried 26 times for 132 yards, scored three touchdowns and kicked three conversions. Syracuse lost, 28–27, because one of Brown's conversion attempts was blocked by a man who charged in while the Syracuse end and fullback were trying to decide who would block him.

Understandably, Jim Brown was voted the game's most valuable player, and Paul Brown agreed. "He was the best man on the field," said the Cleveland coach. "He just about single-handedly propelled his team, even though they were looking for him to carry two or three times on every down sequence."

If the performance pleased Paul Brown, it also must have consoled him for having had to settle for Jim as his first draft choice five weeks earlier.

Coach Brown had gone to the NFL draft meeting with the high hopes of picking a top college quarterback in the first round to replace the retired Otto Graham, who had led Cleveland to ten division championships in ten years before retiring in 1955. But the flip of a coin cost Cleveland its big chance. (The Browns and Pittsburgh, having identical records at draft time 1956, flipped to see who would pick first; Pittsburgh won.)

The first round went like this: On its bonus draw, Green Bay picked Paul Hornung, a top quarterback at Notre Dame. Los Angeles picked halfback Jon Arnett of Southern California. San Francisco picked John Brodie, a top quarterback at Stanford. On its regular draw, Green Bay picked end Ron Kramer of Michigan. Then Pittsburgh picked Len Dawson, top quarterback at Purdue. Thus, three of the first five picks had been top quarterbacks—and had exhausted the supply.

Unable to get what they wanted most, the Browns did the next best thing. They drafted the best player still available—Jim Brown. ("Sometimes," Paul Brown later said, smiling, "you get kicked upstairs.")

The draft did not thrill Jim Brown at the first instant, either. He had wanted to play for the Giants and seemed disappointed when he got the news at school. But he quickly changed his mind as soon as the Syracuse coaches explained that he would have a better chance to play regularly for the Browns because they needed a runner more than the Giants did.

In Jim's previous years at Syracuse, the end of football had meant the beginning of basketball. But, by stretching football an extra six weeks, the bowl game cost him a chance to play basketball again and cost Syracuse a possible national championship. Figuring that the precious practice time he had lost would probably keep him off the starting five, he did not go out. Figuring the same way, the basketball coaches did not beg him to go out. Syracuse finished the regular season with a 16–6 record, won its first two games in the National Collegiate Athletic Association tournament, and then got eliminated by eventual champion North Carolina, 67–58, in a rough game. It is not unreasonable to think that Brown might have made the difference.

Brown kept in shape that winter and continued impressing sports people at Syracuse. "What talent going to waste," boxing coach Roy Simmons said, watching him spar one day. "I am convinced that Jimmy could have been the national intercollegiate heavyweight champion if he had put his mind to it and fought competitively."

"He never played handball, but in his first game he was doing well against our top players," said athletic director Lew Andreas. "The same in wrestling. You name the sport; I'm sure Jim could master it in a short time."

By spring, Jim was ready for lacrosse—and ready to live up to the praise showered on him by Roy Simmons, then in his 26th season as Syracuse lacrosse coach. "Brown is one of the greatest lacrosse players I have ever seen," said Simmons. "He is a fine stick-handler and he can score from either side. As a matter of fact, I think that by comparison Brown is more of an All-American in lacrosse than football."

Sure enough, with Brown scoring five goals in one game against Cortland and six against Rensselaer Polytech, Syracuse sailed along toward its first undefeated lacrosse season since 1924.

On May 15, at Hendricks Field, visiting Cornell got crushed, 22–5, as a midfielder named Jim Brown scored seven goals and five assists. The outburst boosted his season's goals to 42, one short of the national collegiate record, solidified his All-American status, and gave Syracuse its ninth victory in its ten-game season. Only Army, which Syracuse had not beaten in lacrosse in 23 years, stood in the way.

At the other extreme, only Colgate stood between the Syracuse track team and a winless season. Both the track meet and the lacrosse game were scheduled for the same day, Saturday, May 18. In the finest tradition of an adventure series or of Hollywood, this was a job for Superman. Or Jim Thorpe. Or Jim Brown.

Since Brown was closest to campus—and the only one of the three heroes enrolled at Syracuse—he was the logical choice.

Track coach Bob Grieve cleared it with lacrosse coach Roy Simmons, then asked Brown if he would come out of track retirement for one meet. On Thursday, just two days before the doubleheader at Archbold Stadium, Jim reported for track practice and worked out with the javelin and the discus, and in the broad jump and the high jump. After telling a reporter that Brown probably would compete only in the javelin and discus events, coach Grieve admitted that "much will depend on the situation."

(For the record, Brown was not asked by other coaches to compete in the other Saturday events—a baseball game, a golf match, and a crew race. In fairness, though, it must be reported that geographical and time conflicts would have made an afternoon tripleheader impossible. The track meet was scheduled for 12:30, the lacrosse game for 3:00.)

In track, Jim's performance was every boy's daydream come true. He won the high jump (5 feet 8 inches) for five points. He won the discus (139 feet 2 inches) for five points. He finished second in the javelin (167 feet) for three points. Syracuse won by Brown's 13 points, 72–59.

By this time, some 7,500 fans were there, waiting to witness the Final Miracle of Archbold Stadium.

It came to pass.

In lacrosse, ten seconds after Army scored first, Syracuse tied it on a goal by Brown. He was double-teamed the rest of the game and did not score again, having to settle for a tie in his race for the record and the national scoring championship. But his power produced an overwhelming advantage at the center draw, and his passing skill accounted for three assists. Naturally, Syracuse won, 8–6.

The public record of Jim Brown's incredible college career at Syracuse would have ended the moment the lacrosse game ended if publicity man Pinchbeck had not been a baseball fan.

"I wanted to see the end of our game against RPI," said Pinchbeck. "So three of us—a reporter from *Sports Illustrated*, my assistant, and I—went back to my old office in the Stadium. We were sitting there some time later when one of us spotted Big Jim coming out of the dressing room and heading toward the field. As always, he was surrounded by a bunch of kids. The kids dispersed, and Jim started climbing the steps of the Stadium. We had a straight-on view of him, but he didn't see us. I'm sure if he did, he never would have done it. He got to the top and looked over the Stadium for about thirty seconds. Then he sort of waved. I had no idea what he was thinking. Maybe he was saying a sad farewell or maybe he was simply saying, 'Glad this is over,' but he did gesture. It was more of a wave than a salute. I turned to the fellow from *Sports Illustrated* and said, 'I'm glad you saw it. If I ever called you and told you that story, it would be ridiculous to think you'd believe it.'"

Three days later, a Syracuse sportswriter said his hail and farewell to Brown by retelling a story he heard from basketball player Vinnie Albanese.

"Couple of Saturdays ago," said Albanese, "some of us got together for a little basketball in the gym. All of us had played sports on the Hill, and I can tell you we really went at it. There were no holds barred. It was rough and fast . . . up and down the court. . . . After about an hour or so, everybody's tired but we keep going. Then Brownie stops and says, 'Sorry, fellas, but I got to quit. I got to play a lacrosse game.' "

On Monday, June 3, Jim Brown was graduated. He was only a C student, in physical education, but as one of the two marshals for the College of Liberal Arts he led the entire academic procession into the Stadium.

Anyone who guessed that graduation—and a look back at his athletic achievements—might inflate Brown's ego was completely wrong. On the contrary, the very next night, speaking to 350 guests at the All-Sports Dinner in Schenectady, New York, he deftly deflated his overblown image. "I never felt I was good enough in baseball," he admitted, "and just couldn't develop a real interest for it because I thought the action was too slow for me. Incidentally, I want to clarify something that has been said about my high school baseball, where I was credited with two no-hit games. Those two no-hitters came in a summer league I played in at Manhasset, and not in high school play."

More positively, he also praised lacrosse as "a wonderful sport and one in which conditioning is so important in order that a person can have the stamina to go all the way."

That Friday night, Brown was in Baltimore to play college lacrosse for the last time, in a seniors-only, North-South, All-Star game. The game was rated even. The South had momentum and incentive (it had won the two previous years and could take the series lead for the first time in fifteen years), but the North had Brown.

Jack Daut of Rutgers, who had tied Brown for the national scoring championship with 43 goals, started the scoring with nearly 5½ minutes gone in the first period. Then teammate Brown took over. He bounced one goal under All-American goalie Jim Kappler of Maryland and scored twice—unassisted—in quick succession, directly from the face-off. In a little more than two minutes, he had single-handedly raised the North's lead from 1–0 to 4–0. For good measure, he won the face-off ten seconds later, carried the ball downfield and flipped over to Daut, who scored. The North was never headed as it won, 14–10. In all, Brown scored five goals, added two assists, thrilled the crowd of 6,500, and excited two of the top men in college lacrosse.

"Brown is the greatest lacrosse player I've ever seen," said Gardner Mallonnee, a former Johns Hopkins coach and All-American. "And that includes all the great Hopkins and Mt. Washington players I've watched over the last thirty years."

"I've never seen a better lacrosse player," said

Jim Brown as Liberal Arts class marshal at commencement at
Syracuse University, 1957.

Charley Clarke, president of the U. S. Intercollegiate
Lacrosse Association. "It's amazing that a man with
his size can be not only so fast but so graceful. Why,
the way he whirls and dodges is unbelievable."

Yet an opposing coach best explained the frustration

of playing against Brown. "Here," said Jim Smith, "is a fellow who weighs 220 pounds and runs like the wind, and what do they do with him? They give him a stick to hit you with."

A few hours after his last lacrosse triumph, Brown flew to Cleveland and signed a contract to play professional football. It was a fitting climax to a phenomenal college career. Indeed, that was the week that was—a whirlwind.

A capsule summary:

On Monday, he led his class in Syracuse.

On Tuesday, he spoke in Schenectady.

On Wednesday, he spoke in New York City.

On Thursday, he practiced in Baltimore.

On Friday, he led his team in Baltimore.

On Saturday, he signed in Cleveland.

On the seventh day, fittingly, he rested.

CHAPTER 6

Rookie Rampage

IN RETROSPECT, it seems that Cleveland coach Paul Brown could have said little else. He had always liked Marion Motley, the rugged fullback whose hard running and hard blocking had helped the Browns win eight division championships between 1946 and 1953, and he had always disliked going overboard on an untested rookie.

Therefore, when asked before the 1957 season began about the prospects of his No. 1 draft choice, Jim Brown, Paul Brown said: "We hope he will be the next Marion Motley. He has a lot of the same attributes as Motley—size, speed, good running sense, and power. He should get the extra yard and he should hurt opponents when they tackle him, just like Motley did."

Hopeful but cautious. The same words could have been used to describe dozens of NFL rookies of the decade. Yet Jim Brown himself felt even less confident.

"I was worrying about playing with fellows like

Groza, Renfro, and Ford," he recalled. "When I was a kid, I used to have daydreams and say to myself, 'Jimmy Brown, All-American.' I'd finally made that, but this was even more. Here I was with fellows I'd been reading about all my life and idolizing. I couldn't quite picture myself playing with them."

Neither could they.

"We were playing an exhibition against the Lions and he'd just come in from the All-Star game at Chicago," explained Ed Modzelewski, the Brown's regular fullback in 1956. "He didn't know the plays very well and wasn't very sure of himself. He didn't look too good so I figured, 'Well, he's just another challenger.' There'd been others. One kid before Jim—an All-American from Colorado—was supposed to be the greatest thing since penicillin, but they cut him and he went back to selling encyclopedias or something, and I kept playing fullback. So my first reaction to Jim was just that—probably another encyclopedia salesman.

"Then there was another thing going against him," continued Modzelewski. "The law of the jungle. Let's face it. I had a lot of friends on the team. They'd try to hit Jim just a little harder than they normally would hit in practice. But he'd bust out of their arms, and gradually you could see them gaining respect."

The convincer came in one pre-season exhibition game when Brown broke loose and sprinted 48 yards for a touchdown. His teammates became believers and Jim himself once called it "my biggest thrill. Man, that was really it," he said. "I had made it."

On opening day, for his first professional game, he was ready, willing—and able. Against the visiting league-champion New York Giants he carried the ball 21 times, gained 89 yards, and set up the final field goal in Cleveland's 6–3 victory.

With the score tied, 3–3, and one minute remaining in the game, the Browns had possession on their own 42. It was a case of make-it-or-forget it—third down and 14 yards to go. The veteran coach called on the rookie back, and Jim carried the 14 yards for the vital first down. With 21 seconds remaining, Lou Groza won the game with a 47-yard field goal.

For Groza, it was the latest in a long line of heroic actions. For Brown, it was the first—and the most meaningful, especially after he was congratulated by a handful of old-timers that included defensive tackle Bob Gain.

"Gain isn't the kind of fellow who says much," said Brown, "but what he says he means. When he patted my back and told me how well I had run, it meant more to me than anything in the world."

After that impressive start, Jim settled into a four-game groove. On successive Sundays, he averaged 15 carries and 48 yards—not bad, but far from spectacular. Each week, though, he was learning lessons that are taught most lastingly by professional linemen who weigh up to 270 pounds and hit with the speed and force of one-ton trucks. If only to survive, a young professional back soon recognizes the value of such essentials as the quick start, the smooth handoff and the proper way to hit a hole.

"My biggest running fault," Jim admitted later, "was hitting the line with my head down and my eyes closed. Of course, I had to learn that the hard way in a game against the Chicago Cardinals. Our quarterback called the fullback-dive play that we used to pick up a yard or to set up another play. I took the handoff and went into the middle with my head down. I expected to get hit hard, but every man threw a perfect block and I found myself with a clear field in front of me. Then I lost my balance and fell. That cost us an easy touchdown and taught me an important lesson."

Brown quickly changed his running style. With his head up and his eyes open, he was able to see, and to ram tacklers with his more bruising shoulder pads instead of his helmet.

The very next Sunday, November 3, for the first time as a pro, Brown broke the 100-yard barrier. The 109 yards he gained against the Washington Redskins, in 21 attempts, carried him into third place in the NFL rushing race. His 388-yard total trailed only veterans Hugh McElhenny of San Francisco, 419 yards, and Tom Wilson of Los Angeles, 496 yards.

The Browns as a team were doing even better. With the season half over they led the Eastern Division with five victories in six games. The Giants were second with four victories in six games. After a dismal 1956 (only five victories in twelve games), Cleveland was once again enjoying football.

A crowd of 65,407 poured into Municipal Stadium on November 24 to see the game against the Los Angeles Rams, and it seems safe to say that not a single fan—or player or coach or sportswriter—expected the explosion that occurred.

Early in the second period, with the score tied 7–all, coach Brown called for a draw play up the middle. Rookie quarterback Milt Plum and rookie fullback Jim Brown nearly bumped heads, but they completed the handoff. At the line of scrimmage Brown was hit so hard that the ball squirted into the air, but, still undaunted, he caught it two steps later and raced 69 yards—untouched—to a touchdown.

It was a dramatic beginning to a dramatic afternoon.

In the second half, he scored three more touchdowns, plunging over twice from the 1-foot line and once from the 4-yard line.

In all, he carried 31 times and gained 237 yards, breaking Tom Wilson's all-time NFL record of 223.

It was a brilliant one-man performance that far overshadowed the team's 45–31 victory. And it received raves from all corners of the country. Yet one critic did not expect to see too many encores. "If he carries the ball that much in many more games," said Ram coach Sid Gillman, "he's got to wind up either punch drunk or a basket case."

By tradition, a rough, tough athlete like Jim Brown should have laughed loudly—or at least shrugged silently—when asked about pain. But Brown was either so inexperienced or so honest that he actually admitted such a sensation existed. "Every Sunday," he said, "I get hit as hard as a bunch of big, tough guys can hit me. It hurts. It hurts a lot. But sometimes, every now and then, I get away from them. Then I really know that I have accomplished something."

His individual deeds also worked wonders for his team. "The other defenses are concentrating on Brown," explained Tommy O'Connell, Cleveland's starting quarterback. "They key on him. That takes some pressure off me. We've been playing more wide open this year and throwing long more often." By that time O'Connell was leading the league with an average gain of 11.2 yards per pass attempted (2.2 yards better than runner-up Eddie LeBaron), and the Browns had already clinched the division championship.

"This has been my most enjoyable season," admitted perfectionist coach Brown, who seldom admitted happiness during any season. "It's been a pleasure to watch the players get such an apparent joy out of playing. Sometimes it's good to be in an unfavorable psychological position. Starting this season as we did, with people not expecting too much, it made it easier for us to get off to a good start. At first, it was just good defense and Groza's toe that held us up. Then our offense began to roll."

Neither Paul Brown nor anyone else had any way of knowing, of course, but this was to be the peak of his pro coaching career. From the end of 1956 he had gotten "rid of the people who no longer were willing to pay the price," replaced them with fourteen new men, and rebuilt so well and so quickly that he won the 1957 Eastern Division title, his last.

Even though the Browns were nearly blown out of the stadium in the league playoff game (the Western Division champion Detroit Lions won, 59–14), coach Brown had nothing but high praise for fullback Brown.

"There is no question about his tremendous value to us," Paul Brown said in December. "He has a wonderful disposition and he is a leader. He is not one of those windy fellows on or off the field, but he obviously thinks before he speaks and that draws respect."

More important, the coach was willing to compare his present star with his past star. "Brown is not as big as Motley," he said, "but he is as fast off the mark. And we believe he is more difficult to get hold of once you reach him. He is an outstanding player now, and he can be a great one when he reaches his peak."

If any further confirmation of Jim's skills was needed, it came from many sources.

"The best fullback to come into any league in ten years," said veteran scout Jack Lavelle of New York.

"Pro rookie of the year," said the *Sporting News.*

The league's individual rushing leader (202 carries and 942 yards, for a 4.7-yard average and 9 touchdowns), said the NFL.

And in the Associated Press poll of sportswriters for its All-Star team, only one player in the entire league was named on all 36 ballots. He was Jim Brown.

CHAPTER 7

What Sophomore Jinx?

IT HAS been diagnosed as a disease called sophomoritis, treated as a hoodoo called sophomore jinx, and cursed by hundreds of professional athletes who have suffered from it.

But Jim Brown turned out to be totally immune.

In fact, few men, whatever their season, have dominated a professional sport as sophomore Jim Brown dominated professional football for the first half of the 1958 season.

During the first week of summer-training camp at Hiram, Ohio, in late July, Brown surprised the Browns. He was lighter than they expected and faster than they expected.

The first was easily explained. "Army lieutenants don't eat so good," said Jim, who had spent his off season in the service at Fort Benning in hot Georgia. He reported to Hiram at 220 pounds but quickly climbed to his rookie year's playing weight of 228.

The second was easily accepted. In the summer of 1957, he had been working out with the College All-Stars and had missed the Browns' sprints. In the summer of 1958, he was timed at 4.5 seconds for 40 yards, starting from a three-point stance and wearing full football gear. It was the fastest time on the team.

"There is the best draft choice we ever made," said Paul Brown, pointing at Jim Brown one day in early August. Paul said it to a writer once, but he might have been excused if he had said it to himself a few thousand times in the next few months.

In the season's opening game, a 6–3 victory over Los Angeles, Jim rushed the ball into position for the winning field goal, carried 24 times and gained 171 yards. In only one game during all of 1957 (the 237 yards against the same Rams) had he rushed for more than 109 yards.

In the second game, a 45–12 victory over Pittsburgh, he carried less (17 times) and averaged more (7.6 yards) and scored his first touchdown.

The following week, 65,403 fans, the largest opening-game crowd in Cleveland history, showed up to welcome the Browns home and to see for themselves. Jim Brown did not disappoint. He gave the Browns a 14–0 lead over the Chicago Cardinals in the first period by plunging for two touchdowns, later ran 7 yards for a third touchdown, carried 34 times in all and gained a total of 182 yards. His teammate, halfback Bobby Mitchell, helped by sprinting 63 yards for one touchdown and setting up another with a 52-yard run. The Browns won, 35–28.

Amazingly, Jim improved the next two weeks.

Against Pittsburgh again, he averaged 8 yards for 19 carries and scored two touchdowns.

Against Chicago again, he gained 180 yards in only 24 carries and scored four touchdowns.

Cleveland's future opponents finally faced the moment of truth: do something drastic or be buried by Brown.

The New York Giants chose the drastic. They assigned middle linebacker Sam Huff to cover Brown on a man-to-man basis, to key on his every move and to follow him everywhere. It was the beginning of the most publicized man-to-man battle in pro football history—and it worked surprisingly well.

The Giants won, 21–17, while Brown carried fewer times (13) and gained fewer yards (113) than he had in any game all season. Only once, when Huff shifted to the other side of the line, did Brown break away. He dashed 58 yards to a touchdown.

Despite the relatively poor showing against the Giants, Jim's season statistics were staggering. In six games, exactly half a season, he had scored 15 touchdowns and had rushed for 928 yards. The NFL full-season records, both set by Steve Van Buren of Philadelphia, were 18 touchdowns and 1,146 yards.

Brown could have broken the yardage record without playing another game. All he had to do was take all the words of praise spoken and written about him during that half season and stretch them end to end.

A few sample inches:

"He's the best pro back of all time," said Earl (Greasy) Neale, who coached Van Buren for the Eagles. "He's out of this world. I saw three men trying to stop him and he ran right through them. Brown does everything that Van Buren could do as a runner, and then a lot more besides."

"If he's not the greatest runner of all time, he certainly must be as good as anyone has ever been," said Otto Graham, the great Cleveland quarterback who benefited from Marion Motley's brilliant blocking and running for so many title-filled years.

Predictably, the most vivid quotes came from the men who tried to tackle Brown.

"When you hit that guy," said Sam Huff, "he lunges like a bull and sometimes he lunges right out of the tackle."

"He's fast as the fastest, hard as the hardest," said Glenn Holtzman, a 250-pound tackle for Los Angeles. "An arm tackle is no soap; he runs right through you. The only way I've found to stop him is hit him right at the ankles with your shoulder. Otherwise, it's like tackling a locomotive."

Two Pittsburgh Steelers insisted that the biggest problem was Brown's speed. "He's the only player I know," said guard Dale Dodrill, "who can run faster sideways than he can straight ahead." Swift defensive halfback Jack Butler said, "I don't really know how to stop him. I haven't been able to catch up to him yet."

Even once-reluctant Paul Brown jumped on the bandwagon. "Nothing Jimmy might accomplish in football would surprise me now," he said. He also explained the secrets of his star's success. "He has such terrific thigh structure that he hurts tacklers," coach Brown said. "Take a look at that bulge above the knee, even in a pair of two-way stretch football pants, and you notice that terrific thigh structure. He's a strong fellow, starts exceptionally fast and is bigger than he appears to be. He has tremendous ability to do things on his own. Get him in the open past the line of scrimmage and he's liable to run away without anybody in front of him to knock people down."

Probably the quietest man in the league during the Jim Brown excitement was young Steel Thighs himself.

"Jim is a quiet, relaxed human being off the field," wrote Tex Maule of *Sports Illustrated*. "In repose, the magnificent body looks loose, the heavy muscles bulging even at rest, the impression he gives is one of a great hunting cat asleep in the sun. He is not talkative, but he is an articulate young man who understands the technique of running with a football and is able to explain it."

"There are several reasons why I am running better this year than last," Brown told Maule. "First, I fit into the Browns' offensive unit better. I came to camp three weeks late from the All-Stars last year, and for a while

I'd hit the wrong hole on an occasional play. For instance, I wasn't familiar with how Mike McCormack blocks in the middle of the line, and once in a while I'd run into Mike and the man he was blocking because I didn't know which way to cut."

Just when most people writing or talking about the NFL were wrinkling their brows and trying to think of fresh adjectives to describe his triumphs, Jim proved he was human. He was held to 83 yards in 21 rushes, by Detroit.

That relatively poor showing might have been shrugged off as "just one of those things" if it had come during his torrid streak. But it hadn't. His two weakest games had come consecutively, and trend-conscious sportswriters started speculating. Had Jim Brown suddenly slowed down?

"No, I don't think so," Jim Brown told Larry Friedman of Associated Press. "At least I know I'm not doing anything different than I did in those first five games. In those games, I usually had one or two long touchdown runs which made my running average look good. I'm not pressing or thinking about any records. That's something I try to get across to everyone. I just try to do my best every game. Those records will take care of themselves."

Brown, a bachelor who lived alone in a small apartment overlooking a park, then outlined his weekly routine. "There isn't too much time during the football season," he said. "I get up at eight thirty in the morning and have to be at practice at nine thirty. It takes me about five minutes from my apartment. I go to the movies a few times a week, go shopping for clothes and anything else I need, but most of my free time I listen to records. I like music—mostly jazz records, rhythm and blues, some dance tunes, but no classical records. On weekends, it's a different routine. I sleep until noon Saturday, try answering some of my fan letters and get to the hotel with the team at six or six thirty. Then I'm with the fellows until the game. I also read quite a bit, but nothing heavy. Mostly magazines and newspapers. I visit some friends around town quite a bit at night but get to sleep early. Studying plays also takes up some time."

Obviously, his success on the field had not radically changed his personality. He was still thoughtful and courteous to questioners and well-wishers. He signed countless autographs ("When they quit, then I will be worried," he explained) and answered countless calls (until the Browns wisely had his telephone disconnected). But even with the men he knew best, he rarely joked or joined in horseplay. In fact, he talked so seldom that his teammates nicknamed him "Gabby."

In his next game, against Washington, Brown bounced back. He scored twice, carried 27 times, gained 152 yards and pushed past Van Buren's season rushing record with 1,163 yards.

"He's the greatest back ever to come into the league," raved substitute fullback Ed Modzelewski, whose job Brown took. "It's like playing behind Babe Ruth."

If Brown played like Babe Ruth, he sounded like Ruth Jones. "Gee, fine," he said in the dressing room, when reporters swarmed around him and told him he had broken the NFL record. "I just try to move the ball and let the record fall where it may."

Jim's successes came so steadily that it was easy to forget how swiftly he had taken over after his professional debut. In 1957, Modzelewski, the regular fullback in 1956, had his picture on the cover of one stadium program. In 1958, Modzelewski did not even have his picture inside a program.

The first-place Browns were riding high (six victories in eight games) and scoring leader Jim Brown was riding even higher (his 17 touchdowns—one was on a pass reception—included runs of 38, 41, 52, 58, 59, and 60 yards). Both were due for a fall.

The man gained only 66 yards in 20 carries against Philadelphia and only a feeble 12 yards in 11 carries against Washington. He did not score in either game, and the cynics started jumping off the bandwagon.

They blamed Jim Brown for being too tired to run hard any more.

They blamed Paul Brown for working his star too hard too often.

And they credited opposing defenses for ganging up on him. He was, insisted a few, just like those young baseball flashes who hit .400 until they come up against curveballs the second time around.

Again Brown bounced back. He rushed for 138 yards against Philadelphia and 148 yards against New

York. But despite his 65-yard touchdown burst on the Browns' first play from scrimmage, the Giants won that final game of the season (on Pat Summerall's 49-yard field goal with two minutes remaining) and tied Cleveland for the Eastern Division lead.

The playoff game in New York was a bitter battle. But again the Giants won. They shut out the Browns, 10–0, and smothered Jim Brown. He carried only seven times and gained only 8 yards, his worst day ever.

Though the season ended in disappointment, no one could deny that for every game of the first half and for half the games of the second half Jim proved himself one of the most destructive forces in NFL history. In 12 regular-season games, he carried 257 times and gained 1,527 yards. By contrast, the rushing runner-up, Baltimore's Alan Ameche, carried 171 times and gained 791 yards.

Predictably, Brown was again voted the pro player of the year. Predictably, Brown again said, "I'm very proud. But I'd like to give all the credit in the world to the linemen who blocked so well for me all year. They're the ones who made this award possible."

That, of course, was only part of the explanation. Cleveland sportswriter Herman Goldstein pointed out that Brown had (1) taught himself to break away from tacklers and (2) corrected a fault from 1957.

The fault, Brown told Goldstein, was that after starting to move he had the tendency to stop and look and try to pick his way through the defense. "When you do that," Jim explained, "you might beat a tackler

75

but the pursuit will get you. If you stop to cut and get hit, you stop right there. If you're moving and get hit, you may get five yards more. I realize the blockers ahead don't know where you are. They make the blocks the best they can, so it's much better to slash."

Breaking away from tacklers, he explained, was a matter of power and perseverance. "A lot of times," he said, "they tackle you and they think they've got you and sort of let up. If you keep hitting hard, you can often tear away."

The theories sounded sound to Brown fans. But to skeptics, cynics, and non-sycophants they had a hollow ring. After all, in four of his last seven games, he had been held to 83, 66, 12, and 8 yards. He was great while he lasted, they insisted, but he had burned himself out by running so hard so often during the first half of the season.

CHAPTER 8

Ruin at the Top

IF outsiders were convinced that Jim Brown was being ruined by overwork, the man who called on him to carry so often was equally convinced that such complaints were drivel.

"Jimmy has been my No. 1 fullback and he will continue to be," insisted coach Paul Brown before the beginning of the 1959 season. "Any man who has done the job that Jimmy has is entitled to have one or two off days. He thrives on hard work. Just watch. He'll bounce right back."

The coach was correct, and even his worst enemy could never accuse him of not giving Jim a fair chance of proving himself.

After an opening loss to Pittsburgh, Brown carried the ball 37 times against the Chicago Cardinals. Only one man in NFL history had ever carried more in a single game (Harry Newman of New York, 38 times, against Green Bay in 1934).

On muddy Soldier Field that October 4 afternoon, Brown churned for 147 yards rushing (of Cleveland's 160) and two touchdowns in the 34–7 victory. After the game, coach Brown was asked why he had not varied his attack more. He looked at the questioner and icily answered, "Why shoot a popgun when we have a cannon?"

In turn, friends, foes, and men who did not even know him opened fire on Paul Brown. Halfback Tom Wilson, a Los Angeles workhorse whose rushing record of 223 yards in one game had been broken by Jim in 1957, demanded: "What are they trying to do to that man? Nobody can take that kind of punishment and expect to be around this league too long."

An insider much closer to Cleveland, who asked that his name not be used, insisted: "Paul Brown is going to ruin Jimmy Brown. No man, not even a powerhouse like Jimmy, should carry the ball so much. The more he smashes into those big linemen, the more chance he has of getting hurt and ending his career. Sure, let him carry a lot, but at least give him a rest once in a while. He's not a horse. He's only a human being."

Jim Brown let his actions speak. He rushed for a total of 267 yards in the next three weeks. Yet all that was merely a warm-up for his most rigorous test.

On November 1, for the first time in his professional career, he had to face the champion Baltimore Colts. Their mighty line averaged about 260 pounds and included such defensive giants as Gino Marchetti, Art Donovan, Ray Krouse, and a 6-foot-6, 288-pound tackle named Gene (Big Daddy) Lipscomb, "Man," said Lipscomb, "I'm just itching to get my hands on that Jimmy cat." Brown, typically, said nothing.

But he showed up on time, as did the paying crowd of 58,275 fans, at Baltimore's Memorial Stadium. The attraction was the natural that all sports promoters dream about: a battle between the world's best passer, John Unitas, and the world's best runner, Jim Brown.

Despite the dramatics expected, defense dominated the first period. Each team kicked a field goal. Unitas did little. Brown did less, gaining only 15 yards in seven carries.

In the second period, Brown exploded. He took a handoff on the third play, cut inside his right end, and sprinted 70 yards to a touchdown. Minutes later, he drove toward right tackle, slipped through a hole, and ran the remaining 17 yards to another touchdown.

In the second half, he battled the Colts' crunching linemen on their own terms—in hand-to-hand, close-quarter combat. He hurtled across the goal line three more times, on plunges of three, one, and one yards.

For his part, Unitas had a brilliant day. He completed 23 of 41 passes for 397 yards and four touchdowns. But, amazingly, he was overshadowed.

In the 38–31 victory, Brown scored all five Cleveland touchdowns and ground out 178 of Cleveland's 197 yards rushing. He carried 32 times and only once did the Colts as much as stop him for no gain.

"I remember that no gain and a couple of other short carries," Jim said later, chuckling. "I'll tell you, Marchetti and Lipscomb can really hit. When Big Daddy wrapped his giant arms around me, I didn't go anywhere. He stopped me dead a few times."

Big Daddy, understandably, was even more impressed. "I'm afraid I didn't catch that cat as often as I wanted to. No doubt about it. Jimmy is a strong boy and just about the best runner I've ever seen."

Inspired, perhaps, by Lipscomb's praise or simply by Brown's power, syndicated sports columnist Red Smith wryly wrote: "The football record book at Syracuse University reads: 'Most Net Yards Gained, Jim Brown; Most Touchdowns, Jim Brown; Most Points Scored, Jim Brown; Most Yards Punts Returned, Jim Brown; Highest Average One Game, Jim Brown; Highest Average One Season, Jim Brown.' In Cleveland there's another record: 'Most Prayers of Thanksgiving for Jim Brown, Paul Brown.' "

Reminiscing, Syracuse coach Ben Schwartzwalder told Smith: "Jimmy was only sixteen when he came here, a shy boy who didn't mix easily with the others. . . .

"Big Jim used to worry about the delay until he got the ball. It took time before he learned to break at top speed when the play started. Jim had only one big day as a sophomore, you know. He should have had two. The Cornell defense was underslung against us, packed to stop plays to the weak side, so all we had to do was nudge the end out on the other side and send our inside tackle through to take the deep man. Between halves I told our quarterback to do nothing but run Jim off tackle. In the second half, he ran Jim just once, and he went 54 yards for a touchdown. . . .

"Big Jim barely scratched his potential when he was here. I only wish we could have had him around while he matured. In his senior year, he came so fast we couldn't keep up with him—the coaches, I mean. He learned to do many things so well that our thinking never caught up with his ability."

Now, in Jim's third year as a professional, some people said he was faced with a similar plight: a coach who did not know how to use him properly.

The murmurs usually quieted after Cleveland victories that November. The Browns defeated the Philadelphia Eagles; Jim scored twice and carried 29 times for 125 yards, boosting his seven-game totals to 183 carries for 862 yards. The Browns defeated the Washington Redskins; Jim served as a valuable decoy. On Cleveland's first series of downs, quarterback Milt Plum pitched out to Brown, who was swarmed under for a three-yard loss. On the next play, Brown was swarmed under again, but the only problem for Washington was that Plum had merely faked to Brown and had pitched out to halfback Bobby Mitchell, who raced 90 yards for a touchdown. The victory enabled the Browns to tie the Giants for the Eastern Division lead.

Then, on successive Sundays, the Browns lost two games by scores of 21–20 and fell out of first place. The bitterest blow came in early December against the hated Giants.

On one carry in the first period, Jim got tackled so

hard it must have seemed as if half of Yankee Stadium had hit him in the head. "I don't know what play it was," he admitted afterward, "but they told me later I got tackled hard and probably got knocked out on my feet. All I remember is that I was groggy until Milt Plum went to the bench and told the coach to take me out because I was missing my assignments. I sat out the second quarter, even though my head cleared before the half ended, and I went back in the third quarter."

For the first time in nearly a decade of football—high school, college, and professional—Brown had been sidelined by an injury. He found the game grim for other reasons, too. He gained only 50 yards. Yet he might have gained 500 yards and still not been able to carry Cleveland to victory. The Giants won, 48–7.

In team sports, as in war, men are measured mostly by their contributions over an extended period of time. This seems to create a code of heroism that is different from that of individual enterprise. In a close team battle, it is fitting for an injured hero to give his all. But if a team battle is one-sided, it is foolish for an injured hero to be risked at all.

The conquerors cried loudest. "It was a crime to send Jimmy back in after he got hurt," snapped a Giant lineman. "There was no point to it. We had the game wrapped up and that guy was in a daze. He could have got hurt pretty badly. I guess that proves that Paul Brown would do anything for a touchdown."

Paul Brown snapped back. "I'm not in the habit of

asking Giant players what to do in a game," he said. "But I do ask the team doctor, an expert in athletic injuries, before I send any injured player back in. As a matter of fact, the doctor examined Jimmy and said he could go back in ten minutes after he got hurt. We let him sit out the whole period, though, because we didn't want to take any chances."

By the time the season ended, two facts about the Browns stood out.

Jim, as much as ever, was considered the league's top ball-carrier. (In the two wire-service polls for All-Pro, he was the only man named on all 68 ballots.)

Paul, more than ever, was cursed for ruining his star with overwork.

In 1959, Jim carried 290 times (a NFL record) and gained 1,329 yards (second only to his own NFL record). Excluding kicks, his 290 rushes represented nearly two of every five Cleveland plays from scrimmage throughout the entire season.

Yet, as always, the staggering work load did not seem to bother Jim—until the following spring, near contract time.

CHAPTER 9

"It Begins to Tell on You"

"I've run with the ball more than any back in history," said Jim Brown, and nobody had to ask whether he was bragging or complaining.

If there is any subject that can make even the most soft-spoken professional athlete speak up, it is his contract. Honors and awards are nice to receive, he says, but there isn't a grocery store in the country that accepts press clippings in payment for food.

Whatever Jim Brown was earning to play professional football ($22,000 was one estimate), he wanted more. And few people would deny he deserved a raise. But just to make sure, he fired his first volley publicly late in April 1960.

"I haven't signed for next season and unless it is for what I think it ought to be I'll quit," Jim told an Associated Press reporter in Charleston, West Virginia.

"I've run with the ball more than any back in history, and most of my running has been done inside. When they ask you to beat the same spot in the line time and time again, you are running out the clock. It begins to tell on you.

"The coaches in professional football seem to think there is a limit on salaries. I don't. I think a player ought to be paid according to the improvement he shows from one season to the next. If they want to pay me what I'm worth, I may play one, two, even three seasons. But,I'm definitely going to quit soon regardless of what they pay me."

If the threat frightened coach and general manager Paul Brown, he certainly did not show it. "Jim's contract was so high last season that I may have gone overboard," Paul told Cleveland sportswriter Chuck Heaton the next day. "I haven't thought about Jim's contract for next season. Contracts are based on a man's performance, and we haven't completed our studies of last season's games. In any case, we don't do business that way."

Quitting pro football in his prime and supporting Sue, the Southern girl he had married the previous June, would have been improbable—but not impossible—for Jim Brown. He was finishing his second year as an off-season promotion man for Pepsi-Cola and was training for a management position in the marketing division. And he had a long-standing offer of a reported $150,000 to try boxing for two years.

Early in 1958 a Syracuse boxing promoter named Norman Rothschild had offered Jim a $25,000 bonus to sign. He refused. But he listened longer in 1960 when Rothschild raised the offer considerably.

On June 17 Jim ended the suspense by signing a Cleveland football contract for two years. His salary was not made public, but sportswriters estimated it at $30,000 a year. Paul Brown said his star was "being paid in line with being the best running back in the history of the game." He also said he doubted that his star "ever seriously considered a career in boxing."

When asked two months later, Jim did not make it sound so certain. "Norm is a good friend of mine," he explained, "and he named a figure quite a bit higher than $25,000 this time. I'll admit that I gave it a lot of serious thought before I turned it down. It never hurts to listen to a good business deal. After all, when you're playing football you can get hurt or traded tomorrow. Then what do you do? I've got a wife and two kids to support, and I know I won't be able to play football when I'm thirty-five."

Some people insisted that, at the rate he was burning himself out, he would be finished long before that.

Others insisted that, no matter what age he played to, he would not end his career with Cleveland.

"There's no question about it," said a former Cleveland player who knew both Browns well. "When Paul Brown gets hold of a good running back, he rides him to death and then gets rid of him. He did it to Ed Modzelewski and he did it to Preston Carpenter. Now you know what he's doing to Jimmy Brown. Let's see what happens to him when he slows down. Don't forget, no matter how great Jimmy's record is, the Browns have yet to win a championship with him."

That was one insider's opinion, but the author needed more for a story called "Is Jimmy Brown's Career in Danger?" This was not, of course, the kind of blunt question you asked first in interviewing a pro football man. You led with others, then worked into it tactfully.

"Just how strong, really, is Jim Brown?" Sam Huff was asked.

"Well, when he comes through that line, brother, you just have to forget about yourself and dive in there to try and stop him," Huff said in his West Virginia drawl. "You have to hit him from the knees down or you don't have a prayer. Anything from the hips up, he'll either drag you with him or run right over you. Believe me, he's run over me more than once, and it doesn't tickle."

"What about when you do hold his yardage down? How does he react?"

"Jimmy takes it like a real sportsman," said Huff. "I remember one game especially. We stopped him cold on his first carry, and as he got up I hollered, 'C'mon, let's hit him harder.' He carried again and our whole line smothered him. 'C'mon,' I yelled, 'belt him harder.' He carried for the third straight time and again we smothered him. I hollered, 'That's still not hard enough.' This time, as Jimmy got up, he looked at me and laughed. 'Hey,' he said, 'that's plenty hard enough.' "

Then came the key question. "Do you think Jim Brown's career is in danger?"

"I don't know," admitted Huff. "I guess he does get paid pretty good to carry the ball. Of course, no man can get hit so hard and so often without slowing up sooner or later." Sam stopped for a moment. "But I'll tell you," he said, thoughtfully, "if Jimmy Brown has slowed up any yet, I haven't noticed it."

Jim Brown himself was asked if running was really as easy as he made it look.

"I know," he said, "that a lot of people think that all there is to carrying the ball is just taking it from the quarterback and finding yourself out in the open with nobody between you and the goal line. I'm afraid it's not that easy, though. If you hit the line at three-quarter speed like I do, you've got to find your hole before you shift into high gear. Even if the hole is exactly where it's supposed to be, which it seldom is, it can move, and you've got only a split second to slide with it before you get swarmed with tacklers. Remember, it's a heck of a lot easier to run around a man than to try to run over him."

"Who would you say are the toughest defensive players you—"

The question was not completed before Jim started to answer. "I've sure been asked that one plenty of times," he said. "I'd have to name four of them—Lipscomb and Marchetti of the Colts, Joe Schmidt of the Lions, and Sam Huff of the Giants."

"What about the toughest defensive team?"

"No question about that one, either," Jim said. "The Giants. If you'll check the records, you'll see that they've been pretty rough for me."

Indeed, in the five previous Cleveland-New York games, Brown had been held, in yards and carries, to 113-13, 148-26, 8-7, 22-8, and 50-15. He had scored two touchdowns, on bursts of 58 and 65 yards, but he had scored nothing in the last three games. Linebacker Huff had said, "The Browns are only as good as Jimmy Brown. If you can stop him, you can stop them." It seemed to make sense, considering the record. The Giants had won all five games.

"What about it?" Jim was asked. "Do you think you're overworked?"

Jim did not laugh or sigh. He simply sat silent for a few seconds, obviously gathering his thoughts. Then he began to answer. "I get paid pretty good money to carry the ball," he said. "I've never felt that I've carried the ball too much or been worked too hard."

He paused again, then added: "Frankly, I wouldn't mind if they ran me even more. Sure, sometimes it hurts when I get belted going up the middle, but I'm still young enough to take it. I'm going to be twenty-five in February, and I plan to play football as long as I feel I can do a good job."

From there, of course, it was a quick jump to the key question. "Do you think Jim Brown's career is in danger?"

"I feel good and I'm very healthy right now," said Jim Brown. "Of course, nobody can predict the future.

But with a little luck, I should be able to help the team for a few more years."

His reasoning, as usual, sounded logical. "I don't think I'm going to carry the ball as much this season as I have in the past, because we expect to have more balance in the backfield. Milt Plum has gained a lot of confidence at quarterback and should help our passing game. And Bobby Mitchell should do even better than he did last year. [In 1959, halfback Mitchell had gained 743 yards rushing, fifth highest in the NFL behind Brown.] I think he's the best halfback in the league, a real speedboy who can run wild to the outside."

Asking Paul Brown if he thought Jim Brown's career was in danger would have been a bit silly. After all, if Jim Brown was being overworked it was only because Paul Brown was calling his number too often.

The only diplomatic thing to do was to remind the coach that Jim had rushed 290 times in 1959 and to ask what plans he had for 1960.

"Jimmy will probably carry the ball less this year," said Paul Brown. "But I can assure you it won't be because anybody thinks we're endangering his career. It's just that we've got more balance on offense than we've had in the last three years."

Both Browns turned out to be prophets. On offense, not one, not two, but three men bore the burden and balanced the attack.

Bobby Mitchell caught 45 passes for 612 yards and rushed for 506 yards more.

Milt Plum led the league in passing for the first season ever. He completed 60 percent and averaged 9.2 yards gain every time he threw. And Jim Brown—despite a badly bruised ankle in the first game that troubled him all year—led the league in rushing for the fourth season in succession, the first man in NFL history to do it. He carried 215 times and gained 1,257 yards, pushing his four-year yardage total to 5,055. (Marion Motley, by comparison, had rushed for 4,712 yards in eight years.)

Powered by the triple-threat offense, the Browns scored more points than any other team in the league. But in the vital victory and defeat departments, because of a relatively weak defense, they finished only second best (8–3–1) to the Eastern Division (10–2) and league champion Philadelphia Eagles.

The major consolation for Cleveland came in the season's final game, December 18, when the Browns and the Giants fought it out in New York for second place in the Eastern standings.

The Giants had won six straight in the two-team series and seemed certain to make it seven because of what happened before the opening kickoff. Jim and six teammates stepped into an elevator on the sixth floor of the Concourse Plaza Hotel and suddenly, almost literally, got the ride to end all rides. The car went out of control and plummeted to the basement. Fortunately, no one was hurt, and the Browns walked the three blocks to Yankee Stadium.

It was a bitingly cold day, and the Giants were

rather hot. They carried a 34–21 lead into the final period. Worse yet, for Cleveland fans (and there were few of them in the crowd of 56,517), Brown had carried only seven times and had gained only 25 yards.

Finally, after 27 long quarters of frustration against the Giants, the Browns exploded. First, Plum threw his fourth touchdown pass of the game, 37 yards to Brown. Next, a runback of an intercepted pass put Cleveland ahead, 35–34. Then an abortive run-instead-of-punt play gave Cleveland possession again on the New York 45. Brown ran 19 yards, teammates combined for 15 more, and he ran for the final 12 and a 42-34 lead. And lastly, another runback of another intercepted pass ended the scoring in the 48–34 upset.

The next day, at a New York Quarterbacks Club luncheon in Leone's, Jim Brown was smiling as he said, "I can look Sam Huff in the eye today."

Reminded of his rivalry with Huff, Brown told a story about a time he attended a sports banquet in up-state New York. "They handed out fancy programs with thumbnail sketches of the speakers," he said. "In mine, it had my fondest wish being to run over Sam Huff. I got up and said that was wrong. My fondest wish is to stay as far away from Sam Huff as possible."

Later, someone in the audience asked how the Browns shaped up for 1961. (In 1960, 12 of the team's 38 men had been rookies.)

"We have a great group," said Brown. "This year of experience has done our rookies a tremendous amount of good." He then praised Plum and other teammates and admitted, "I feel better when I'm running the ball a lot."

A few hours after finishing a full season, he sounded as if he were ready to start a new one. And considering his past and his team's future, who could blame him?

CHAPTER 10

The Man and The Money

*It's reached a point where our best defensive men run
off the field, waving and shouting for joy, "I touched
him. I touched him."*

—KYLE ROTE, New York Giants

JOKING about Jim Brown got to be the big thing
for opponents on the banquet circuit. Most had little
choice. They had run out of adjectives and they still
couldn't stop him on the football field.

Before the beginning of the 1961 season, though,
Rote's recently retired teammate, Frank Gifford—himself a solid running back for nearly a decade—was
asked for a serious rating of the NFL running backs.

Gifford called Brown "the greatest running back
ever" and, aided by writer Dick Kaplan, filed the following report in *Sport* magazine:

94

Believe everything you've heard and read about this amazing, indestructible, once-in-a-lifetime football player. He's the perfect blend of balance, bone-crunching power and unbelievable speed for a man his size. What he can't run over, he outruns. Brown's program weight is 228 pounds, but my buddies on the New York Giant defensive unit swear that he's closer to 240—and hits like a ton. Jimmy can plow into a bunch of tacklers and literally move the pile back by sheer, brute force. You have to see the game films to believe your eyes. . . .

The big difference between Jimmy Brown and every other fine fullback in the NFL is that nobody ever catches him from behind. He can transform a routine three-yard gain into a spectacular, 70-yard scoring run—and outrun every linebacker around, almost all the defensive halfbacks and more than a few offensive scatbacks. . . .

But Jimmy isn't only fast. He's a classic example of what I call "intelligent speed." For example, Brown rarely hammers into the line head-down at maximum speed. He decoys the defensive linemen into believing he's got the throttle pulled all the way out, then, just as the hole opens, he shifts from controlled three-quarter speed into all-out overdrive and leaves them embracing empty air. And if the hole is plugged when he reaches the line of scrimmage, Jim has a fantastic knack of sliding off tacklers while he searches for an alternate opening.

Yet while people talked about Jim Brown, Jim Brown talked about Paul Brown—and not always admiringly.

"Paul Brown is a lot more than a coach in Cleveland," Jim said. "He signs you to a contract, he coaches you on the field, he tells you what to eat and he tells you when to get up and go to bed." Jim objected to the rigid routine of training camp and to the coach's habit of calling all the plays from the sideline. "I'd like to see him relax a bit," Jim said. "He could call 90 percent of the plays and let the quarterback have a little fun."

It was far from scathing criticism, but it was, significantly, the first time the player publicly suggested that the coach was injuring team morale. It was not to be the last time.

But once the season began, Jim concentrated on carrying the ball. He had little time each Sunday to do anything else.

In an early game against St. Louis, he was the only Cleveland back—except for quarterback Plum, of course—to carry the ball in the entire first period. Equally shocking, of Cleveland's first 13 plays from scrimmage (excluding punts), he either rushed or was Plum's passing target 12 times.

"Did you ever use Jim Brown more at the beginning of a game than you did today?" writer Myron Cope asked coach Paul Brown after the 34–7 victory.

"Yes," snapped Brown.

Cope persisted, pointing out the 12-of-13 figures and

implying the obvious—that if Brown's answer were true, he would previously have had to use Jim 13-of-13 times.

"When you got a big gun, young man, you shoot it," snapped Brown. He offered no further explanation.

The next day, for *Sport*, Cope called on Jim Brown at his small white-frame house with green trim. Jim, wearing black slacks and a black polo shirt, was standing in the rain and punching holes in his lawn with an aerifier. He walked into the house, sat down, and said: "That was a very satisfying game yesterday. I was tired and weak—my body went weak. It was hot out there and we were all tired and weak, and the only thing we had left was our heart, but we didn't give up. Lot of satisfaction from that."

During his visit to Cleveland, Cope learned about Jim Brown the man from a teammate, from a neighbor, and from the man himself.

"My beliefs are simple," said Jim, when asked about religion. "I believe in a Supreme Power and in treating my neighbors right. If you stick to those beliefs, there's not too much wrong you can do. I am a Baptist, but I don't believe other religions are wrong. The differences in religions are *man's* interpretations."

About movies, Jim said: "I enjoy foreign movies, mainly because their portrayal of life is more realistic."

About books, Jim said: "I don't like to take a man and say he's my favorite author. A man may write one book that's good and another that's not so good."

About the football public, Jim said: "Attention and

autograph collectors don't bother me. The public are the ones who support you. You should be glad."

"You'd never know he was a big celebrity," said a neighbor, Dr. Clifton Hines. "He's just a neighbor—we talk about how to get the grass to grow better."

As a neighbor and a friend, however, Dr. Hines couldn't help noticing Brown's wardrobe. "He has shoes on top of shoes, hats on top of hats and suits on top of suits," the physician said. "He had a derby once that he wore, and I called him The Diplomat. He said, 'You know, Doc, you just haven't got nerve enough to wear one.'

"One of the first things he does when he comes in the house," continued Dr. Hines, "is turn on his record player. He'll play it as long as he's there—and loud."

Among other things, Jim at that time liked progressive jazz, rock 'n' roll, and show music. He also liked to startle his teammate and close friend, Bobby Mitchell —a prime source for the few funny stories in existence about Jim Brown.

"One day," said Mitchell, Brown's roommate on the road and in training camp, "he took that infant boy of his to the barbershop for a haircut. You know how kids hate that, but Jim's boy was a perfect little gentleman and Jim was busting proud of him. The next day, we're in the middle of a football game and Jim had just caught a screen pass and made a beautiful move on a halfback and gone 50 yards.

"He comes back to the huddle and first thing whispers to me, 'You know, that little fellow of mine is really something. He lays down on the floor and you can't move him. He's strong as an ox.' "

One night in Los Angeles, Brown and Mitchell were racing back to their hotel room to beat the curfew—and the accompanying fine of $250 each. They reached the hotel elevator, rode up, then dashed down the corridor, just as assistant coach Ed Ulinski was checking rooms. Ulinski quickly stepped aside as the two-man herd thundered past.

"In the game next day," Mitchell recalled, "Jim had just run over some guy—smacked him real hard—and he comes back to the huddle, crouches down, and says to me, 'You know, if Ed Ulinski hadn't a-got out of the way he would have got hurt, 'cause for $250 I'd have run over him.' "

Brown's opponents knew the feeling.

In a 17–6 victory over the Redskins in Washington, on November 12, he carried 20 times, gained 133 yards, and pushed his way into second place as a career ground-gainer in the NFL. The leader, Joe Perry of Baltimore and formerly of San Francisco, had gained 7,246 yards in eleven seasons. In eight seasons, Steve Van Buren of Philadelphia had gained 5,860 yards.

In four and a half seasons, Jim Brown of Cleveland had gained 5,908 yards.

But after the game he seemed most excited about the way the coach called the plays. "He went into the game with an open mind," Jim said. "There was deception and surprise." Indeed there was. One of Cleveland's two touchdowns came on a 37-yard pass thrown by none other than Jim Brown.

The following week in Cleveland, against the same Philadelphia Eagles who had defeated them on opening day, the Browns played as if they had only one more day on earth to reap revenge. And Jim Brown played as if he were trying to catch up with Joe Perry in one afternoon.

Jim gave Cleveland a 7–3 lead in the second period by bucking over from the 2. After Philadelphia scored again, Jim scored again. His 4-yard run for a touchdown gave Cleveland a 14–10 lead.

In the third period, Cleveland moved farther ahead, 24–10, on Milt Plum's 28-yard touchdown pass to Bobby Mitchell and Lou Groza's 17-yard field goal.

In the fourth period, both teams opened their offensive valves wide. The Eagles scored twice (on passes by quarterback Sonny Jurgensen). The Browns scored three times (on Mitchell's dash of 91 yards and Brown's drives of 1 and 8 yards). The Browns had clinched a 45–24 victory, Mitchell had scored two touchdowns and Brown three, but in the closing minutes a contagious excitement swept through the Cleveland crowd of 68,399.

"Go, Jim, go!" the chant began, and the more Jim went, the stronger the chant grew.

With two minutes remaining, pressbox statisticians calculated that, to tie his own NFL rushing record of 237 yards in a single game, Jim needed only 13 yards.

Plum took the snap from center, pivoted, and handed off to Brown. The fullback surged ahead; the Philadelphia line surged back until all the bodies in motion came to rest 7 yards from the line of scrimmage. Twice more Plum pivoted and twice more Brown pushed ahead—first for 4 yards, then for 7 yards. The public-address man announced a new record of 242 yards, and the crowd roared.

"I glanced up at the scoreboard," Brown said in the dressing room afterward. "I thought maybe Pitt had beaten New York."

"Do you know what your old rushing record was, Jim?" asked a reporter.

"No, I don't," Jim said, and who would have expected him to say anything else? "I know it's over 200 yards, though."

He was told his old record was 237 and his new record was 242. Then came the question of the ages— what does the record mean to you?—and the inevitable answer.

"Oh, it's nice, but nobody cares if you don't win," Jim said. "And I knew we'd win this one. Knew it when we left the hotel. We were sky-high."

"Isn't thirty-four carries too many?" asked a reporter. "Can't that shorten your career, like a pitcher going too many innings?"

Jim nodded toward Paul Brown and said, "If he says carry fifty times, I carry fifty."

When asked if that had been his best game, Jim either spoke with a forked tongue or one sportswriter supposedly there was being bothered by a buzzing in the ear.

A Cleveland writer quoted him as answering: "I won't say this was my best game. I've played some better all-round games this year. I missed a few blocks today. And a couple of times I went the wrong way when I got a good block. The blocking was tremendous. No, I don't think I ran any better than usual."

A Philadelphia writer quoted him as answering: "I think so. I picked my holes, used my blocking better."

If the sportswriters were divided in their opinions, the Eagles were unanimous in theirs.

"Finest one-man performance I've seen," said losing coach Nick Skorich.

"He hit those holes so fast I didn't even see him go by," said defensive tackle Jess Richardson. "He seemed to want to hurt us."

That intent was fully realized, according to Eagle defensive back Bobby Freeman. "Jimmy tore us up," admitted Freeman. "There is no runner in the league to compare with him. When you think you have Brown stopped for a yard gain, he ends up with five or six."

The next morning, the official scorer added two cents of his own and subtracted five yards of Jim's. In rechecking the rushing totals, the scorer admitted, he discovered that Brown had gained only 237 yards (the word "only" sometimes seems so inadequate) and had only tied his own record.

Jim took the news about as hard as if he had been told that a recheck revealed the day's attendance was actually 68,394 instead of the 68,399 first reported. "The fact that we won the game is the main thing," he explained. "If it had been someone else's record that had stood for several years, it might have meant something."

The way his mind was working was revealed best when someone pointed out that Jim had been smiling more that season. "I have been enjoying it," he admitted. "This is a fine group of fellows. Spirit is good." Then he made a point publicly that would take on much stronger significance a year later. The lift in team spirit, he implied, was due largely to the actions of new owner Art Modell. "He takes personal interest in the players," said Jim. "Win or lose, you find him in the dressing room with a handshake." By contrast, coach Brown had never been noted as a good loser.

Except for the fact that Cleveland traded veteran star Bobby Mitchell to Washington for the Redskins' first draft choice, halfback Ernie Davis of Syracuse, the rest of the regular season followed what had become known before 1960 as the usual script. The Browns faltered against the Giants and lost the Eastern Division race; Jim Brown won the rushing title. His official figures were 305 carries for 1,408 yards (a 4.6-yard average) and 8 touchdowns.

Informed that he had won his fifth consecutive championship, Jim said, "It's been a long season, but there's real satisfaction when I think I was able to come through it without injury."

He was not to be so fortunate the next season, or even so formal the next month.

"It was my roughest year in football," he told Los Angeles sportswriter Mel Durslag in January. "It was my feeling last season that I was asked to do more than my share. I made more than 300 rushes and caught 46 passes. Obviously, the club planned to trade Bobby Mitchell, a great runner and flanker. So I was given many of his plays. I never objected to doing my bit, but I don't care to take the burden to help a trading scheme on the part of the club."

Durslag asked if Jim objected to Paul Brown during the season, and Jim said, "No, I didn't. When I'm out on the field, it is my place to do what the coach says. If he keeps calling my plays, I perform to the best of my ability. My time to object is when the season ends and a new contract is presented."

That time had come, of course, and Jim seemed to be looking far beyond a new contract. But unlike 1960, when boxing threatened to steal pro football's finest runner, business was the lure in 1962.

"There is a very important job that may be coming up for me," he said. "There is an emphasis these days on special markets. By that I mean the Puerto Rican market, the Spanish market, or the Negro market. People are aware of company's representatives in these fields. For the representatives, it can be very lucrative work. If this job comes through, it will allow me to make the transition from football to business at no loss of income. And, of course, it will allow me to build something for the future. I have had five years of pro football. Now I should start to think of something more substantial."

His announcement did not exactly shock coach Paul Brown. "This is the time of the year for our Jim to start laying the groundwork for a new contract," he said, crisply. "He is a great player and we expect him to be playing again as usual."

In Miami Beach, the man who shook his players' hands, owner Art Modell, sounded much more sympathetic. "There must be a misunderstanding somewhere," he said. "As far as [loading work on Jim] being part of the scheme, I have to say that this is not so. That trade came about very late in the season. I was under the strong impression Jimmy likes to carry the ball as much as possible. I just don't understand this."

The difference in attitudes between Modell and Paul Brown became even more obvious as Modell continued talking. "Certainly," he said, "Paul Brown and myself will sit down, talk to Jimmy and try to persuade him he has a lot more football left. I like the man very much. If he decided not to play any more, it would be a great loss to the league, the Cleveland Browns, and the public at large. . . . I'm sure he would be happy to play with us another year."

The skeptics who agreed with Paul Brown that Jim was bargaining now for higher pay later were saying "I told you so" the next week. Back in Cleveland, Jim told sportswriter Chuck Heaton that the employment people at Pepsi-Cola "are interested in having me play for a few more years. It would be pretty hard for me to give it up. I still love to play football."

He was available, apparently, if the raise was right ($10,000 was one estimate), and he saw no reason why it wouldn't be. "I never have had any contract difficulties and I can't see any reason why there would be trouble this time," he said. Then, as if to reassure himself, he ticked off the following four points:

"I played out my two-year contract, including the two extra games this season, without asking for any additional money.

"The Browns have had a good home attendance since I've been here, and with the extra home game the 1961 season may have been their best.

"Basketball may not be a big money-maker most places, but a fellow like Elgin Baylor makes his $50,000.

"With Bobby [Mitchell] gone, I'm the only veteran among the running backs."

He did not press the point, but the Browns had paid Ernie Davis, an untested rookie, a three-year package of some $80,000. It almost went without saying, therefore, that Jim Brown, the greatest running back in history, deserved a sizable increase over his estimated annual salary of $32,000.

Yet as winter wore on, and he traveled the banquet circuit, it became clearer that money was not the only object of Jim's disaffections.

"I don't see how getting rid of the best breakaway

runner in the league can help us," he said in Jamestown, New York. "I think Davis will be a good, solid player, but he'll never be as spectacular as Mitchell. I think it was a mistake to trade Mitchell, particularly before the season was over. When we played our last game, Bobby knew he was gone. Two good men are involved in the deal and they're both friends of mine. Nobody will know how it works out until next year."

In mid-February, Jim was joined by teammate Milt Plum in publicly criticizing the Cleveland system. The fact that coach Brown called nearly every play from the bench instead of allowing his quarterback to check off (change the play at the line of scrimmage because of defensive shifts), complained Plum, "hurts spirit and morale. I compare us to an auto with a top speed of seventy miles an hour. We can't go any faster no matter what the situation. The team is in a rut. We don't get up for the big games most of the time and often have a struggle with the not-so-strong teams."

Jim supported Plum. "I think Milt gave constructive criticism that was well thought out," he said in Philadelphia. "I think that his only thought was in helping the ball club and letting Paul know some of the feelings of the players. . . . I think it was really constructive criticism if anything. Plum was never able to call a checkoff."

But, alas, it was one thing for a super-star like Brown to criticize and another thing for a merely good player like Plum to do it. The month after his "constructive criticism," Plum was traded to Detroit.

Finally, in late May, Jim signed a Cleveland contract for an estimated $42,000, assuring him of being the highest-paid player in pro football. Many people had expected just that kind of climax to his complaints, and, in fact, Jim sounded like an ideal organization man. He signed, then said he was "looking forward to having a fine year" and planned to "give 100 percent, as I always do."

For his part, Paul Brown said, "We hope he has the kind of year that a contract like this would call for."

On the contrary, it was to be a year filled with frustration.

CHAPTER 11

Speaking Out

IT FIGURED.

The Browns opened the 1962 season by defeating the Giants, and from that pinnacle there was only one way to go. By the time the season ended, though both were much more disappointments than disgraces, the key question was: Who had fallen farther—the Cleveland Browns or Jim Brown?

Having traded 195-pound Bobby Mitchell for 215-pound Ernie Davis to get a bigger backfield or, more specifically, a 1–2 power punch like Green Bay's Jim Taylor and Paul Hornung, Cleveland's first frustrations came in July. Davis was hospitalized with a blood disease, which was diagnosed as leukemia. (His tragic death the following May deprived him of playing a single minute of professional football.)

Yet Tom Wilson, 205 pounds and able to run inside and outside, filled in at halfback and provided the running balance that powered Cleveland to a 17–7 victory over New York on opening day. Wilson carried 18 times and gained 76 yards; Brown carried 17 times and gained 134 yards. "It was an outstanding success," Jim recalled later. "We had a better running attack than ever before. Actually, we beat them on the ground."

From then on, the situation slowly worsened for all the Browns—Jim, Paul, and players. Soon after the season closed, Cleveland sportswriter Hal Lebovitz sat down with Jim, and the pair produced a penetrating analysis of the sad comedown of the Browns. Their story from *Sport* is quoted freely in this chapter.

In evaluating the second game, against Washington, Jim said: "I did the same amount of running, but Wilson wasn't used too much. In the first quarter, I threw a stupid lateral and they raced it back for a touchdown. In the final minutes of the game, when we were ahead 16–10, I fumbled in a crucial spot, just when we were eating out the clock. They recovered and set up Bobby Mitchell's touchdown that beat us. I always said that was my individual loss. I lost that game. I'll take full responsibility."

The following week, against Philadelphia, Jim did not get much of a chance to redeem himself. He was called upon to carry the ball only 12 times, and he gained only 38 yards. Wilson worked even less. That game, according to Jim, was "the turning point."

"We suddenly completely forgot about the balanced offense that we had been using, the stuff that had been so successful," he said. "We forgot about the spread and the double wing [formations]. I never could find out why. We went to throwing almost completely and we were whomped. As for myself, when I don't carry much, I don't do much."

The Browns rebounded and defeated Dallas the following week, 19–10, but it was similar to winning the battle and losing the war. In the first period, as he was being tackled, Jim jammed his left wrist or, more probably, had it jammed by an opponent. He had it taped and continued to play.

Week after week, he played with a pained wrist and without a complaint. Since professionals have been known to go after an injured player with the express intent of weakening a weakness, all the Browns kept Jim's secret. Not until after the final game did Dr. Victor Ippolito, the team physician, reveal that the injury had been a severely sprained wrist, which had caused a great deal of swelling and pain.

"Even at the end of the season, although it had improved, there was still swelling and discomfort," said Dr. Ippolito. "He never complained. We thought it might be broken, but we couldn't get him to come in for an X-ray for a week. I finally insisted. There was no fracture. We treated it with ice and pressure and wrapped it for each game, sheltering it with foam rubber. With a wrist like that, the tendency for the player is to protect it."

Hands. It does not require genius to realize that an athlete who loses the use of one hand loses at least half his effectiveness. Sonny Liston, a man-mountain con-

111

sidered indestructible by many people, sat on his stool and gave up his heavyweight championship because he could not lift one hand. But Jim Brown played every game for a full season.

For years, he had carried the ball in his left hand and swung full force at tacklers' chests or stomachs with his right hand and forearm.

For most of 1962, he had to carry the ball in his right hand and carry his left hand helplessly at his side.

"You can see in the movies where in one game, just out of habit, he transferred the ball from his good hand to his bad one, and it squirted right out," said teammate Lou Groza.

After practice one day, Jim suggested a game of golf to Ernie Davis. "I'll give you ten strokes," said Brown.

"You'd beat me bad," said Davis. "I haven't played for some time."

"C'mon, Ernie," insisted Brown. "I can only play with my right hand."

"You mean," asked Davis, "you don't even put your left hand on the club?"

Brown laughed. "Look, I can't even close it," he said. "I keep my left hand at my side. C'mon, I want to take some of your bonus money."

They went and Jim, playing one-handed, won.

But greens and golf balls don't hit back. Linemen and linebackers do. And the advantage they have over a one-handed ball-carrier is vital in a game that often separates success from failure by inches.

Because Brown feared that people would interpret it as an alibi, he refused at first to talk about his injury. Finally, after considerable prodding by a good friend, writer Lebovitz, Brown admitted the seriousness of his handicap.

"Your hands," Jim said. "This is what you make it with as a back. A back has to handle the ball, catch the ball, push away tacklers. The hand is an essential part of your equipment. The biggest trouble comes through natural contact even though you try to keep it immobile. Makes it hard to heal. I'm not hiding behind my hand—I don't want it to sound that way. Anyone with common sense realizes a man doesn't play football one-handed. It's like a bird with one wing."

It is, of course, not necessary to devote days to defending the season that Brown had in 1962. True, he failed to win the rushing championship for the first time in six seasons. And true, he failed to gain 1,000 yards for the first time in five seasons. But he did

—Finish fourth in league rushing (996 yards on 230 carries) behind the new champion, Jim Taylor (1,474 yards in 272 carries).

—Finish third in league scoring (108 points on 13 touchdowns running and 5 touchdowns receiving) behind Taylor's 114 points.

—Fill opponents' hearts with respect, if not fear. "He's the best fullback God ever made," said Giant tackle Dick Modzelewski after the final game. "They can't compare him with Jim Taylor or anybody. I've tackled Taylor myself. To bring down Brown—and

I'm talking about the Brown of '62—I needed the help of the whole defensive line plus Sam Huff. In general, the Browns' offensive blocking is good but not the greatest. Put Jimmy Brown on our team, with our offensive pattern, and he'd be unstoppable. If the NFL exists another two thousand years, there won't be a fullback as good as him."

And Brown accomplished all this for a third-place team with an offense as predictable as any pro team's in modern times. On big plays, Jim almost always carried up the middle because, besides him, the backfield men were either inexperienced or unable to equal their predecessors' success. At quarterback, Milt Plum, who led the league in passing in 1961, had been traded and replaced by Jim Ninowski and Frank Ryan, who finished fourteenth and fourth, respectively, in 1962. At halfback, Bobby Mitchell had been traded to Washington (where he led the league in pass receiving) and replaced by Tom Wilson, who, in turn, had been replaced by others less effective.

"I always wondered why Wilson didn't play more," said Brown. "When did we look good? When we had the combination, the balance." He explained that when Wilson was benched (because, some said, he had offfield problems that affected his play and his relationship with Paul Brown) before mid-season, the team reverted to "the old Mitchell offense, except we didn't flip to the halfback the way we did to him. So now we had a stereotyped offense, the old offense without the flip. The reason was we had no set halfback."

114

In eight of fourteen games, this limited attack was held to 17 points or less. Only by owning the strongest defense in the Eastern Conference were the Browns able to win seven games and tie one, their second-worst showing since Jim joined them at the start of 1957.

Films of different games began to look like reruns of the same game. "That linebacker was right in there, following Jim like a hound dog," said veteran tackle Bob Gain. "If Jim headed for an opening in the line, the linebacker was waiting. He had nobody else to worry about. Look at the movies. Sure the linebackers covered him to some degree in other years but not as completely. They had Mitchell to worry about. He could ruin you."

Yet if Brown was concerned with the drop in his personal statistics, he hid it well. "Yardage isn't the big thing," he said. "Winning the championship is. One thing you learn from gaining yards is that you don't think about them. They come. This is an integrated part of the attack. Sometimes they're abundant, sometimes scarce. It really depends upon how many times you carry the ball. Even from a financial point, yardage doesn't mean much. The championship means about $6,000. That's what I work for—winning the championship."

He had publicly expressed the same feelings many times before. Many professional stars had. But Jim Brown, a super-star whose thinking stretched beyond the following week, felt compelled to go beyond the grumbling that usually accompanied a team's dissatisfaction. He spoke out as strongly as any thoughtful athlete ever did. And he specifically lashed the highly restrictive, impersonal system commanded by coach Paul Brown.

"There's nothing to gain by keeping quiet any longer," he told Lebovitz. "What happened this year is not a one-year story. It's been a six-year story for me. A couple of years ago, I said I was dissatisfied with the organization. Then Arthur Modell came into the picture as the new owner. He brought in a warm, human element and I started enjoying it here. But the way the situation is now and through no fault of his, I don't know if I can enjoy it any longer or give them their money's worth.

"I'm the kind of player who must perform freely, be relaxed. It's no good to play under a feeling of tension, of suppression of the individual. I like to have freedom of expression, a give-and-take of ideas. Under our coaching system, everything is supposed to be automatic. After so many years, it's an established fact that a player should know a little about the game. When this isn't recognized, you feel hopeless.

"This is the way I've always felt, whether I personally gained 1500 yards or 500. The only reason I'm speaking out now is that if I'm going to continue to play under this organization it will have to be with the understanding that I'll be more free. I have to express myself and if I can't have this understanding with the coach it's his prerogative to trade me. I know when

116

Milt Plum spoke out at the end of last year he was gone not too long afterward and maybe I'll be taking the Milt Plum train, too. As I say, that's the coach's prerogative. Under the present atmosphere, I'd just as soon take my chances elsewhere.

"A running back has to feel inspired, to feel free to make moves without worrying about the consequences. He has to feel confident enough and relaxed enough to use his own moves. If he becomes a mechanical man who is told how to step and where to step, he may perform without mechanical error but without too much greatness.

"What I'm saying is what a number of others have felt. Some said it privately, others openly. Bobby Mitchell always was afraid of making an error when he was here. He was quoted as saying he never seemed to be able to please Paul. He wasn't sure of his starting position. A fumble and he'd be benched. In the case of Milt Plum, it was the same. He never felt self-confident.

"The facts speak for themselves that certain players whose ability never was brought out here are now doing outstanding jobs for other clubs. Look at the Green Bay roster. I feel this way: in order to attain the success we're capable of, we must have more of the human element, a closer relationship with the coach, more spirit and less emphasis on minor detail. The way it is now, there's nothing to look forward to. The situation is in the worst state now it's been in my six years here.

"I don't want this to sound like a crying job. Whatever I've done wrong, I'll take full responsibility. The natural mistakes are made by the individual, regardless of the system.

"I'm highly paid. I get along tremendously with the owner, Arthur Modell. I'm not bawled out too much or criticized by the coaches. When I've got it coming, I expect it. I like my teammates. The newspapers and fans in Cleveland have been wonderful to me.

"I want this on the record.

"My frustration is not because of any individual problem. Personally, I have been treated well. I'm definitely not happy because as a team I don't feel we accomplished what we should have. That's the whole thing. It doesn't seem we've done everything to win the championship. We haven't taken advantage of our potential. I'm willing to remain with the Browns, but if I do I want to feel we're all on the right track."

On January 10, 1963, after 167 victories, 8 ties, and only 53 defeats in 17 seasons as coach of the Cleveland Browns, Paul Brown was fired.

"He probably has made more vital contributions to the game than anybody in history," admitted owner Modell, who did the firing. "It was the toughest decision of my life."

"Morale-wise," said Jim Brown, "I think things will improve with the team. Players don't like to be treated as inferiors."

It figured.

CHAPTER 12

"Everybody's on the Same Page"

YEARS ago, one popular song insisted that Saturday night was the loneliest night in the week. That song might never have been written if the lyricist had sat in the stands of Cleveland's Municipal Stadium on the Saturday night of August 17, 1963. A crowd of 83,218 turned out to see a pro football doubleheader. Both games were merely pre-season exhibitions, but one of them was also the Browns' first game in Cleveland under new head coach Blanton Collier.

After eight minutes and 53 seconds of play in the first period, one voice in the stands suddenly rose above the rest and issued a clarion call. "Bring back Paul Brown," it demanded, and before the night was over others were urging the same recall.

The Browns lost to Baltimore, 21–7, and looked worse than the score indicated.

In the dressing room after the exhibition, Jim Brown

spoke out once again. This time, he was practically pleading. "Don't quit on us," he told the writers. "Give us a chance. We have a lot of new things and it takes time to get squared away."

Then coach Collier went to work. An assistant under Paul Brown from 1946 to 1953 and again in 1962 (he coached the University of Kentucky in between), Collier was just as dedicated as Brown, but far less didactic. He asked for suggestions and showed his players he was interested in their ideas. He built Frank Ryan's confidence at quarterback, helped improve his passing, and gave him the opportunity to check off. And Collier installed the option blocking made famous by the Green Bay Packers.

Under Paul Brown, the linemen were forced to block only in the direction they were assigned. Under option blocking, they were allowed to block their opponent either in or out, depending on their relative positions on each play. This, in turn, gave the ball-carrier the option of cutting inside or outside.

"Blanton gives us the opportunity to play instinctive ball," Jim explained. "In this way, you aren't a robot. You can use your head. I glance at, say, three men and know there's an area I should aim at first. On option 6, I'll look at the tackle's block to see what's happening. If the tackle has the defensive end in a bad way, I'll head off his block. If it's congested, I'll glance inside or outside and may make a sweep out of it."

By opening day, the Browns were vastly improved—on land and in the air. They crushed the visiting Washington Redskins, 37–14. Place-kicker Lou Groza kicked three field goals and four extra points. Quarterback Frank Ryan completed 21 of 32 passes for 334 yards and two touchdowns. And then there was Jim Brown. He carried 15 times for 162 yards, caught three passes for another 100 yards, and scored three touchdowns. But how he scored them. One was a rather routine 10-yard sweep around left end; the other two were tremendously exciting—an 80-yard sprint with a pitchout and an 83-yard sprint with a screen pass.

"He gave one of the greatest exhibitions of running you will ever see," said grateful coach Collier.

"The blocking was very good," said grateful star Brown. "There were a lot of men downfield in front of me."

Both explanations were readily accepted by grateful Cleveland fans. They knew full well that in pro football it matters not how you play the game—only whether you win or lose.

After ambushing the Redskins, the Browns went to Dallas and did the same to the Cowboys, 41–24. In nearly 100-degree heat in the Cotton Bowl, Groza kicked two field goals and four extra points. Ryan ran for one touchdown and threw for two more. But again both were overshadowed by Brown.

Near the end of 1962, Jim had carried only eight times and had gained only 29 yards in an entire game against Dallas. But this was 1963, a new season under a new system and a new coach.

Early in the second period, Brown drove toward

tackle, burst through an opening, sped into the secondary, and raced 71 yards for a touchdown.

Late in the fourth period, he hit a little closer to the center of the line and ran a little less, but the 62-yard touchdown was worth the same six points.

Since Cleveland did not get the ball again, Brown settled for 232 yards—only 5 short of his NFL record —in 20 carries. As usual, the victory seemed to please him most. "Everything's been going just fine," he said. "I just hope things keep going this way."

As usual, his teammates were delighted with Jim's success. "I'm proud to block for that guy," said 255-pound tackle Dick Schafrath. And, as usual, the losing coach could not say enough about the man who beat him. "I have no doubt but that Brown is football's finest runner of all time," said Tom Landry of Dallas. "It's all in leg drive. Brown's tremendous. He won't go down until you put him down. He is very fast and has great balance. Once he gets a step on the secondary, no one can catch him."

Then, prophetically, Landry added: "He will probably have his finest year since he is running outside so much, something he never did before."

The following week, against the visiting Los Angeles Rams on a rain-soaked field, Groza kicked two extra points and Ryan threw two touchdown passes. Brown was more steady than spectacular. He scored once, on a 17-yard run, carried 22 times, and gained 95 yards. By contrast, the Rams rushed for a total of 85 yards. The Browns won their third straight, 20–6.

Soon after the game ended, the skeptics started talking. They demanded to know how anybody could get excited about the undefeated Browns since they hadn't really played a tough team yet. It was a point, of course. Among them in 1962, the Redskins, Cowboys, and Rams had won only 11 of 42 games. Just wait till the Pittsburgh Steelers arrive, the skeptics warned.

The Pittsburgh game was October 5, and once again Saturday night was far from the loneliest night of the week in Cleveland. A staggering total of 84,684 fans —the largest crowd in Cleveland football history— jammed their way into Municipal Stadium. Most of them were not disappointed.

After Pittsburgh's opening field goal, the Browns got the ball on their own 18 and moved swiftly. In six plays they covered 74 yards—49 by Brown—to the Pittsburgh 8-yard line. Then Brown charged into the middle and over the goal line.

Early in the third period the Browns were behind again, 20–14, when they took over on their own 23. This time Jim made his 49 yards in one play, racing around left end and cutting toward the middle. Moments later, from the Pittsburgh 20, he surged off tackle to the 13. With a third down and 2, the Steelers understandably were set to stop Brown on a power play. But instead of handing off, quarterback Ryan kept the ball and ran. "I just followed Jim," Ryan explained later. "Their attention was on him. I slipped by. I was only after two yards, but I went all the thirteen for a TD."

Cleveland went on to a 35–23 victory, and the skeptics went silent. It was just as well. They never would have been heard in the clamor that preceded the Cleveland-New York game. Thousands of fans were talking about it, and dozens of insiders in both cities were asked the specific reasons behind the brilliant starts of both Brown and the Browns. The most enlightening answers came from some of the men most responsible.

"The whole thing is attitude," linebacker and captain Galen Fiss told talented reporter Hal Lebovitz. "That's the biggest thing. Here's an example. On the plane trip to Dallas for our game with the Cowboys, everybody had their playbooks out and about 90 percent were talking football. Nobody told them to. They did it on their own because they wanted to.

"Why the change? Because we have a part in the planning. We suggest plays and to a certain extent design some of our own. Blanton asks for suggestions. Of course, nothing is added without his approval, and he refines our ideas if they are accepted. Ryan and Ninowski take movies home every night, mostly movies of the team we're going to play, and they come back with play ideas that might work against them.

"We're working harder at thinking about improving our game, rather than about a specific club or specific individuals on the opposition. We think about it more on our own, away from the practice field, than we ever did before.

"All this is because to a certain extent we're more responsible for what we're going to do. The offense is calling its own plays. The coaching staff does make suggestions and plays are called down from the roof, but the quarterback calls most of them on his own and therefore he has to give this a lot of thought.

"There hasn't been as great a change in the defense as in the offense, because we always called our own defenses. Even so, we're more together now. We're more concerned with the offense and its problems, and they're more concerned with ours.

"As Blanton says, it's our club. The responsibilities are ours. We have a democracy now. He's more than willing to listen to ideas. He solicits our suggestions. He wants us to take an active part in the thinking as well as the playing.

"So you see the system now is altogether different. Before, they did the planning and we carried it out. Now we're involved in the planning and we want to be right."

"I feel people do better when they join in and help plan a thing and are part of it," explained Collier. "They're men, not kids. Their families are dependent on what they do. They've had football experiences, plenty of them, and I feel it's wise to take advantage of these experiences."

The new system stimulated all the players, but none responded with more enthusiam than Jim Brown. Though he had never given less than 100 percent when called on to carry the ball, he began contributing much more at all times.

"Jim is a completely different person this year," said a teammate who did not want to be identified. "He talks it up in the huddles and on the bench. He takes an active interest in the defenses, showing a real interest in their problems. And he's always complimenting the offensive line for their good blocks. He feels that's what the guys need. He's taken charge—almost like a captain on offense, a leader.

"In other years when he was given the game ball after a game he'd say, 'Thanks.' That was about all, although you could see he appreciated it. This year I've heard him make speeches in the locker room. Something like, 'All we've got to do is believe and stick together.'

"And after practice he used to head right for the locker room. Now he'll do a little extra running around the field. He doesn't need it for himself because he's always in top condition, but it's like he's setting an example for the others. He realizes now more so than ever that the things he does mean a lot on the field. He realizes he can help spark a practice.

"He carries us. There's no question about it. We all know this. If he congratulates us, it's as good as the coach doing it."

Even such a seemingly insignificant matter as Jim's running harder than ever in practice produced a beneficial chain reaction.

"This kind of thing rubs off on the rest of us," explained another teammate, linebacker Vince Costello. "When the backs run hard, this steps up the tempo for everybody. The blockers have to block harder and the defense has to hustle more, and the quarterback has to be sharper."

The inspirational extra effort that Jim was exerting was easily attributed to the coaching change. When asked if 1963 was starting out to be his most enjoyable season, Jim said: "Yes, I'd have to say so. I imagine this is so because I'm more or less free and able to participate and able to communicate. Everybody around me is able to do so. There are no undertones. Everybody feels free to think things out and to bring them out.

"We feel now it's accepted," he continued. "All of us now have a feeling for this. We have the same goal. It's not a phony thing. It would be funny to be here six years and sit back and do my job and make no other contributions, when contributions are welcomed. Blanton set the pace. He had to encourage us to participate.

"In the past, it basically was a one-man show. Now it's a team effort. We're together."

Collier, of course, taught more than togetherness. "Blanton knows as much about techniques as anybody I've ever met," Jim said. "The word for him is knowledgeable. I actually learned how to run the 6 and 7 offtackle and sweep on his coaching. He got me rolling into them, rather than slanting. I could handle them much better after taking his advice."

Jim was told that some people said he was playing extra hard to try to show up Paul Brown.

"That's ridiculous," he said. "Anybody who says

that is a small-minded person not worth paying attention to. What would that get me? I don't even think about Paul. I now have the opportunity to do what I believe in. I don't look back. I prefer not to talk about the past. I've always given my best even when I didn't believe in what I was being asked to do. But I always felt there were ways to make them work better and now, thanks to Blanton, I have the opportunity."

In New York, the attitude of some of the Giants was typically professional, but rather funny. It was almost as if they believed that if they didn't think much about Jim Brown, he might disappear.

"He's just a number in the backfield," said defensive back Dick Lynch. "That's the way [defensive end and coach Andy] Robustelli wants us to think."

"We're not going to set up any special defense to stop Jimmy Brown," said coach Allie Sherman. "We can't afford to focus our defense entirely on one man. If that broke down, we'd be through."

But Sherman did not disguise his admiration. "Brown's the best, certainly in my time," Sherman said. "When you go for him, you got to go for him good. A lot of people think that what Brown does he does just on his physical attributes. But that's not so. I learned that when I had a chance to coach him in the Pro Bowl game. He makes some fine moves. He's bigger, stronger, and faster, sure, but it isn't just that. He knows what he's doing. He knows it all the time."

Sherman's predecessor as Giants' coach, Jim Lee Howell, recalled the time he also coached Brown in a

Pro Bowl game. "I was going over some pre-game basics in the dressing room," said Howell. "I had decided to put two men on the opposition's linebackers and was at the blackboard illustrating the maneuver when Brown, still a rookie, spoke up:

" 'Coach, that might be a waste of manpower. I'd suggest . . .'

"Now, at the time I was already an old hand at this business, enjoying fairly good success with the Giants, and so I was rather taken aback. A fresh guy, I said to myself. One of those clubhouse lawyers. Audibly, and none too sweetly, I asked, 'All right, young man, just what do you think I ought to do?'

" 'Coach,' he said, 'instead of putting those two men on the linebackers, put them on the line and if they can open holes, even little ones, I can get through and score.'

"All the time Brown was talking, I was studying him. His sincerity, eagerness, and competitive confidence were unmistakable. Besides, the more I thought about his suggestion, the better I liked it. We put the two men on the line, they opened holes—big ones and little ones—and Brown had himself quite an afternoon."

Howell called Brown the greatest fullback he had ever seen, and sports columnist Joe Williams of the New York *World-Telegram and Sun* asked what made Brown so extra-special.

"Power and speed," said Howell. "Plus exceptional balance. He's the hardest runner to knock off his feet in football. And he makes remarkable use of his hips.

129

You might say this is his secret weapon. He rolls and pivots with tacklers, shakes them off, staggers when hit, but unless it's a good one, or he's two-timed, he'll stay up and keep going without breaking stride."

Williams mentioned the statistical success the Giants had had against Brown, but Howell urged: "Do us a favor and don't print those details. We don't want to give him any ambitious ideas about Sunday."

On the team bus taking the Browns from their New York hotel to Yankee Stadium Sunday, the players were extremely quiet. Before the game, well-liked Ray Renfro, a player-coach, spoke briefly. Later, he told Brown: "You do more by your example than all the speeches I could ever make." Judging from Jim's performance that day (detailed in Chapter 1), Renfro was right—and then some.

"They tried to face-tackle him, but a lot of times it was a punch," Renfro said afterward. "But he never said a word."

All Jim did in the 35–24 victory was catch four passes for 86 yards, carry 23 times for 123 yards, and score three touchdowns. He caught one more pass in the dressing room, when Cleveland captain Galen Fiss tossed him the game ball. His teammates cheered mightily, and Jim's face was wreathed in smiles.

"It's an over-all thing," Jim said, when asked again for a specific reason behind the Browns' surge. "There are so many factors it's ridiculous to try to pin it down. There are the coaching ideas. The balance of passing and running, the variety. We used to sit on a lead or go into a shell protecting a lead. Now we'll pass more. Now it's hard to categorize us. We pass or run at any stage of the game. There's more halfback blocking than we had. Downfield blocking of the receivers. But the main thing on the field is the blocking of the line.

"I don't play any different," he continued. "It's just that everybody else is doing more. Everybody's on the same page. We're all in unison and knowing what we're trying to do."

When pressed about his personal surge, he said: "I'm very happy to be able to utilize everything I have. I like to run outside and I like to run inside. I like to have a two-way go."

Whatever the reasons, the undefeated Browns—with five consecutive victories—were in first place, and Jim Brown—with 787 yards, an amazing 7.8-yard average per carry—was making a farce of the National Football League rushing race.

The same Sunday that the Browns crushed the Giants, the Philadelphia Eagles rallied and defeated the Washington Redskins. But, going home on the train to Philadelphia that night, some of the Eagles were already looking ahead one week to playing Cleveland. The conversation, of course, centered on the man —or Superman—of the hour.

According to sportswriter Sandy Grady of the Philadelphia *Evening Bulletin*, their words went like this:

"Hardest I've ever seen him hit," said Maxie Baughan, "was by Gummy Carr. The ball went one way and Brown went the other. It shook him up, but Brown didn't say a word."

"Yeah, but then he'll go back to the huddle sorta slow," said Tommy McDonald, mimicking Brown's mournful, plowboy shuffle after a play. "You can hear him say, 'Oh, hell,' like he's really tuckered out. Then the next play—vrooom!"

Tom Brookshier began laughing. "Remember how Joe Robb used to attack Brown? I mean attack him. He'd claw and scratch and bite, anything to stop Brown. One play, old Joe and somebody else hit Brown outside real good. They tore off his jersey and cursed him and knocked his helmet sideways and racked him good. Next play, Brown goes into the middle—it's about five yards for a touchdown—and you see this whole mass of people moving real slow toward the goal. Ol' Jim's down under that pile like a tractor, moving everybody with him."

"I hope some of these rookies don't see The Big Horse undressed," said one veteran. "Brown's the only guy who looks bigger without pads than he does in 'em. Very bad for morale."

"Worst thing about that big monster," Brookshier said, "is that awful speed. I chased him about 60 one time and didn't gain a lick. I kept hoping somebody would block me so I wouldn't look so silly."

"He's always been super," Tim Brown said, "but this year Mr. J. B. must be super-super."

"Maybe guys sat around the railroad coaches of

forty years ago and talked this way of Thorpe," wrote Grady. "When a fellow gets his teeth rattled loose by J. Brown, he figures he should send his denture to the Hall of Fame."

The allusion was not all that farfetched. About that time, Eagle safety man Don Burroughs said: "Every time I tackle Brown, I hear a dice game going on inside my mouth."

Going into the game against the visiting Eagles, Jim needed only 51 yards to break the all-time rushing record of 8,296 yards, held by Joe Perry of San Francisco. Brown broke the record with an 8-yard carry in the second period, then finished the afternoon with 144 yards and a new record of 8,390 yards.

"It doesn't mean a thing yet," he said, referring to his record after the 37–7 rout. "Nothing counts until the championship is won."

At a Cleveland Touchdown Club luncheon the next day, Jim explained: "Our game plan was to run a great deal, because they had injuries to their defensive line regulars. In the dressing room before the game, I talked to several of our internal linemen about the importance of sticking with it. Well, Gene Hickerson is one man who doesn't always run quite as fast as he can in practice, and sometimes I find myself close to colliding with him. But Gene said, 'Jim, I'm really going to drive and hit today. I'm going to try to knock somebody's head off.' It gave me a tremendous lift to hear Gene say that."

Another of Brown's blockers, end Gary Collins, who

also caught three touchdown passes against the Eagles, had a different explanation for driving at the defense men. "I had to get out of Jim's way," said Collins, laughing. "He was coming right at me, and looked like a freight train. I told him, 'Don't you run toward me like that. I want to live a while.'"

All the jollity disappeared quickly that week, while the Browns prepared for their return game against the Giants. The Browns knew that their undefeated record of six straight victories would only force the defending conference champion Giants to fight harder.

"I expect it to be another rough game," Brown said. Well aware of the physical punishment he had taken two weeks earlier, he also said: "I don't jaw at anybody, but I don't particularly plan to let anyone take advantage of me."

A crowd of 84,213 poured into Cleveland's Municipal Stadium that October 27. As the game turned out, seldom have so many sat so long and cheered so little.

The first time Brown carried, on the second play of the game, the Giants' giant tackle, 280-pound John Lo-Vetere, hit him so hard the ball shook loose and Sam Huff fell on it. Seconds later, Don Chandler kicked a 29-yard field goal and the Giants led, 3–0.

Almost immediately after the next kickoff, the Giants intercepted a Cleveland pass. They quickly completed one of their own, Y. A. Tittle to Del Shofner, for 23 yards, a touchdown and a 10–0 lead.

By half time, and by playing almost perfect football, the Giants led, 23–0. Their offense was crisp, their defense almost incredible. Time after time, the linebackers blitzed or the front four put on so much pressure that the Cleveland offense was helpless. Brown carried only six times and gained only 35 yards, and quarterback Ryan found the going even rougher. He threw nine times, completed only one but lost six yards on it.

By the end of the third period, the Giants were almost out of sight, 33–0, and any chance the Browns got they threw. Finally, with six minutes remaining, substitute quarterback Jim Ninowski and end Tom Hutchinson combined on a 70-yard desperation pass play that moved Cleveland to the New York 10. Two plays later, Ninowski fired to Rich Kreitling for a touchdown. To add insult to injury, Sam Huff blocked the conversion attempt.

At 33–6, the game was decided. But both teams battled on. With 58 seconds remaining, and the Browns trying another pass, Giant linebacker Tom Scott crashed into blocker Brown and hit him with a forearm in the face. Brown wrestled Scott to the ground, and the officials broke it up. Both fighters were ejected from the game.

It was Brown's first fight; indeed, it was the first time he had ever expressed emotion publicly in a pro game. Yet he was not about to talk about it afterward.

"The only thing significant that happened out there today was the Giants won the ball game—that's all," he said, when reporters asked about the fight.

Other Cleveland people felt the same way.

"The Browns were up for six weeks in a row, and at

times the emotional well runs dry," said coach Collier. "The men wanted to play and tried to get themselves ready. The Giants' offensive and defensive lines out-charged us. In fact, they outplayed us in every department. Nothing I say should be construed as an alibi or an excuse. New York was more inspired, hit harder and played very well."

"A funny thing happened on the way to the championship—we got moidered," wrote Bill Scholl of the Cleveland *Press.* "For six games, it was like a high, fast ride on a jet. Then the floor of the plane fell out."

The tailspin continued.

Against the same Eagles they had crushed by 30 points two weeks earlier, the Browns had to hang on for a 23–17 victory. The result would have been much worse if Lou Groza had not kicked three field goals, and Jim Brown had not gained 223 yards in 28 carries.

Against the Steelers they had defeated by 12 points, the Browns lost, 9–7. The margin was a safety scored late in the third period when Pittsburgh linebacker Bob Schmitz stopped Brown's forward motion behind the goal line. The play was a pitchout that began from the 3, and Brown offered no excuse. "I just got trapped in the end zone," he said. "That was all. How dangerous a play is depends on how the breaks fall. They didn't fall right." The defeat, coupled with a Giant victory, created a tie for first between New York and Cleveland.

Against the St. Louis Cardinals, the Browns lost again, 20–14. This defeat, coupled with another Giant victory, created a tie for second place between St. Louis

136

and Cleveland. Each had seven victories and three defeats. New York was first, with eight and two.

The tailspin was no laughing matter. Thus, a remark by Ed Henke, a veteran defensive end for St. Louis, did not draw too many chuckles. Asked how to stop Brown, Henke said, "Tackle him above the waist and holler for help, or he'll drag you to death."

Luckily for the Browns, their next opponent was the Cowboys. Cleveland won, 27–17, and climbed into a three-way tie for first with St. Louis and New York.

The following Sunday, December 1, quarterback Ryan regained his passing poise and had his best afternoon in six weeks. He completed 10 of 18 passes for 210 yards and, equally important, spread the St. Louis defenses. With adequate running room, Brown carried 29 times, gained 179 yards, and set a season rushing record of 1,677 yards.

He passed his previous NFL record (1,527 yards in 1958) in a dramatic play in the first period. With Cleveland on its own 3, third down and 14, Jim burst past the blitzing linebackers on a draw play, cut to the sideline and raced 61 yards before being knocked out of bounds. "That was a big play," Cardinal coach Wally Lemm said later. "It took the Browns out of the soup." Cleveland won, 24–10, and remained in the race for its first conference championship since 1957.

But the Detroit Lions turned a dream into a nightmare. They clawed Cleveland in Tiger Stadium, 38–10. Brown probably said it all when he said after the game, "We just got the heck kicked out of us. Period."

137

In the season finale, the Browns defeated the reliable Redskins, 27–20, clinched second place, and helped Brown become the first pro in history to run more than a mile in one season. He finished with 1,863 yards—more than the rushing yardage of eleven of the league's remaining thirteen *teams*—and the overwhelming respect of his opponents. He was voted, by the league's players, the league's most valuable player.

"It'd certainly be nice to have him in our backfield," said Y. A. Tittle of the division champion Giants. "I said last year after the Pro Bowl game, he convinced me that third and five is not a passing down any more."

On January 12, 1964, in Los Angeles, Brown played in his seventh Pro Bowl (All-Star) game in his seven seasons as a pro. His East team lost to the West, 31–17, and he did not win the Player of the Game award, which he had done in 1963 and 1962. But he did score two touchdowns and gain 101 yards rushing, the highest total in the game.

And, most important, he said he had no immediate thoughts of retirement.

"I'm happy," he said, in the same city where he had sounded off in 1962. "I've had complete cooperation from management. When the time comes [to retire], maybe in a couple of years, I'll do it with complete understanding and agreement with the owners, coaches, and other officials. Right now, I'm looking forward to coming back out here next year and helping the East to win."

CHAPTER 13

After Six Lean Years . . .

JIM BROWN did go back to Los Angeles in January 1965 and he did play for the East in his eighth straight Pro Bowl, but he might just as well have stayed home. The West not only won its fifth game in six years but also handed the East as bad a beating as any team had ever received in the series, 34–14.

Historians, however, won't even waste a footnote on that game because, after six lean years, 1964 was the year the Cleveland Browns finally won their conference championship. Then, for good measure, they crushed the Baltimore Colts in the NFL title game. Not co-incidentally, 1964 was also the year that Jim Brown did not have to do it alone.

The Browns began functioning as a full team of talent in their very first game of the season. Against the Washington Redskins, in rain-soaked D.C. Stadium, Cleveland quickly fell behind, 10–0. But the visitors' alert defense fell on four Washington fumbles, the offense marched close enough to let Brown plunge for two touchdowns from the 1 and the Browns won, 27–13.

Cleveland came from behind again the following week against the visiting St. Louis Cardinals. Trailing 30–26 with 90 seconds remaining in the game, the Browns broke from their huddle and trotted to the line of scrimmage for what could well have been their final chance—fourth down and 19 yards to go on the St. Louis 45. But flanker Gary Collins made a brilliant catch of quarterback Frank Ryan's desperation pass on the 2. Two plays later, with 48 seconds left, Jim Brown swept right end for the go-ahead touchdown.

Even though the Cardinals, amazingly, stormed back and kicked a game-tying field goal, the Browns had given a good indication of how their attack would be balanced most of the season: perennial placekicker Lou Groza booted four field goals, rookie end Paul Warfield caught one touchdown pass from Ryan, Collins caught another and Brown, carrying 21 times for a mere mortal's 79 yards, rushed for one TD.

In Philadelphia, Cleveland came from behind for the third consecutive week. Down 13–7 at half-time, the Browns rode Ryan's right arm for three second-half touchdown passes (24 yards to Warfield, 12 yards to Collins and 40 yards to Brown) and won, 28–20. Halfback Ernie Green raced 37 yards for the first score and Groza kicked the four points-after. The Browns— all of them—were off to a swift and successful start.

In the 27–6 victory over the Dallas Cowboys, Ryan hit Green, Warfield and Collins with TD passes, Groza kicked two field goals and, doing its part, the Cleveland defense blocked not one but two field-goal attempts. Jim Brown? Again he acted like a mere mortal, carrying 23 times for 89 yards, but again he contributed at least that much more just by being there.

After the game, Dallas linebacker Chuck Howley explained why. Howley, troubled by minor injuries in the first month of the season, had finally returned to action in the second half and had come on strong—knocking down one pass, intercepting another and tackling the passer for a 5-yard loss. "I'm just glad they didn't pass right at the start of the half," Howley said. "By the time they did, I had gotten used to being out there again. But in the beginning, all I could think of was Jimmy Brown."

The specter of Jim Brown continued to haunt his opponents even on those rare occasions when they managed to stop him in the flesh.

The visiting Pittsburgh Steelers held Jim to a season-low of 59 yards rushing and upset the Browns, 23–7, behind the three-touchdown thrust of veteran fullback John Henry Johnson. That night of October 10, Johnson carried 30 times and gained exactly 200 yards rushing, the ninth man in NFL history ever to reach that select circle. "It was the best game I ever had," said Johnson, yet comparisons of his finest hour were inevitable. Jim Brown, the only NFL player ever to hit 200 more than once, had done it four times.

141

Cleveland, now with a 3-1-1 record, bounced back fast from its first defeat. On the opening play of the next game, fullback Brown startled the crowd in the Dallas Cotton Bowl by sprinting 71 yards to the Cowboy 3. Two minutes later, Green slashed over for the touchdown, and Cleveland continued on to a 20–16 victory.

Similar explosiveness buried the New York Giants the next Sunday. After leading only 14–13, the Browns burst through for 28 points in the final period, romped 42–20 and gained sole possession of first place in the Eastern Conference. Seldom had there been a better example of a "team victory." The Browns intercepted three passes, recovered three fumbles and spread their six touchdowns among six different players—Leroy Kelly, Paul Warfield, Paul Wiggin, Gary Collins, Charley Scales and Johnny Brewer.

On November 1, it was four other fellows' turns. Lou Groza kicked three field goals, Ernie Green ran for two touchdowns, Clifton McNeil scored once and Jim Brown drove through and around the Pittsburgh line 23 times for 149 yards, raising his career total to 10,135. He was now the first man in the league ever to rush for more than 10,000 yards, but at boom times like this the individual is always secondary to the team. Cleveland had won, 30–17, avenged its earlier loss to the Steelers and, most important, had taken a two-game lead over the runner-up Cardinals in the Eastern race.

When Washington came into Cleveland, some of his fans were happy to see former Brown Bobby

Mitchell score a couple of touchdowns, but the overwhelming majority were delighted to see the Browns win their fourth straight, 34–24. Mitchell's close friend, Jim Brown, had a pretty good game, too. Despite an injured toe, which was to bother him the rest of the season, he rushed for 121 yards, scored one touchdown and passed to Collins for another.

A crowd of 83,064 poured into Cleveland Stadium on the 15th and roared often as the Browns came from behind twice and beat the Detroit Lions for the first time ever in regular-season play, 37–21. It was much older hat about Jim Brown, but they enjoyed his performance, too—two touchdowns and 147 yards, which raised his season total to 1,081. It was the sixth time in his eight seasons that he had topped 1,000 yards, yet only the 21st time that any NFL player had done it in 45 years.

As usual, his exploits touched off another volley of exclamations. "The big man was really running big today," said Lion linebacker Wayne Walker. "He almost tore my arms off several times." And two Browns with vastly different degrees of personal exposure to their top teammate came to similar conclusions.

Paul Warfield, an offensive end in his first pro season, said: "I have been watching Jim play since I was a freshman in high school, and I always thought he was great. But now I see him practice, too, and he has taught me that striving for perfection in practice enables you to be far superior in game action. Jim has certainly helped me correct my faults."

Paul Wiggin, a defensive end in his eighth pro season, said: "Jim Brown is our team's No. 1 source of inspiration. His great second effort not only spurs our offense but radiates to the defense as well. I am happy he is on our side, not only because his determined running wins games for us, but also because I personally get to watch him run in every game he plays."

Two weeks later, after a loss to the Green Bay Packers and a win over the Philadelphia Eagles, Jim Brown and the rest of the Browns came to the crucial part of the season. If they beat or tied the Cardinals in St. Louis, the Browns would clinch their first Eastern Conference championship in seven years.

Despite Cleveland's tremendous team play all season, many people sized up the big game the way former Brown Floyd Peters did right after his Eagles had fallen to Cleveland. "Both defenses are about the same. But on offense the Browns have the big guy [Jim Brown]. He's the difference. Take today's game. The Browns got ahead of us 21 points. How do you defense them with that lead when they have a horse like Brown? He keeps you from putting too much pressure on the passer. If you rush Ryan, Brown gets the handoff and he's gone. If you play Brown, Ryan has time to pass."

Peters' reasoning was clear but incomplete. He neglected to mention what might happen if the Cardinals leaped into a long lead. That, of course, is just what happened. Trailing 21–3 in the second period, the Browns were forced to concentrate on passing. Jim gained only 12 yards rushing in the second half, St. Louis won 28–19 and Cleveland had only one more chance—beat the Giants in New York.

It was the final game of the regular season. If Cleveland (9-3-1) won the game, it would win the title no matter what second-place St. Louis (8-3-2) did against Philadelphia. If Cleveland tied the Giants and the Cardinals won, a playoff would be needed. And if the Browns lost and the Cardinals won, St. Louis would win the title.

As matters turned out, the Cardinals wouldn't even have had to play on Sunday, December 13. The Browns settled it on Saturday the 12th. In front of 63,007 fans at Yankee Stadium, Cleveland quarterback Frank Ryan completed 12 of 13 passes, including five for touchdowns, and blew down the Giants, 52–20.

One of Ryan's scoring passes went to Jim Brown. It was a short play—only 7 yards in all—but a rather historic one. In the third period, Brown caught the ball on the New York 5, faked rookie linebacker Lou Slaby out of the way and dashed into the end zone for the 105th touchdown of his pro career. No man had ever scored more.

In all, it had been another outstanding season for Brown. He was the only man in the league to repeat as an individual champion, winning the rushing title (280 carries for 1,446 yards) for the second straight year and for a phenomenal seventh time in eight years. But this time, he had had more help than ever. He—and the Browns—had:

Halfback Ernie Green, who blocked well when he wasn't running 109 times for 491 yards and six touchdowns;

Quarterback Frank Ryan, who bloomed as a signal-caller and led the league with 25 touchdown passes;

Newcomer Paul Warfield, who finished fifth in the league with 920 yards receiving and ninth with 52 catches;

Old-timer Lou Groza, who tied for second place in the league scoring race with 22 field goals and 49 conversions for 115 points;

And a strong spirit spread around by such veteran defensive standouts as captain Galen Fiss, Vince Costello, Bill Glass and Dick Modzelewski.

Because of the balance, Jim Brown at last had another chance at the sole goal he had always insisted he worked for—"winning the championship."

Sentiment aside, however, the Browns were the decided underdogs.

In previous title play, the Browns had lost four of their seven games, their last being that lopsided loss of 59–14 to Detroit in 1957. The Western Conference champion Baltimore Colts had won their only two tries (23–17 in 1958 and 31–16 in 1959, both over New York), and the West had won six of the last seven championship games.

On the basis of 1964 play only, the Colts again had to be favored. While winning 12 of their 14 games, they had led the league in total offense (4,779 yards rushing and passing) as well as accomplishing the enviable double of scoring the most points and allowing the fewest.

Though the Browns had led the league in touchdown passes, the Colts had excelled in pressuring the passer. Indeed, the Colt defense had dumped opposing quarterbacks 57 times for 489 yards lost, both league highs. By contrast, Cleveland had accounted for the league lows in those two categories, catching quarterbacks only 28 times for 222 yards. And, as everyone was well aware, the Browns would be facing the coolest quarterback in football, John Unitas.

December 27, 1964 was a wintry, windy, cloudy, cold day in Cleveland, but 79,544 fans poured into Municipal Stadium expecting to be warmed by the offensive fireworks. And no wonder. The 1964 Colts had scored more points (428) than any other team in NFL history except the 1950 Los Angeles Rams (466) and the 1963 Giants (448). The 1964 Browns (415) had tied the 1962 Packers for fourth in that all-time ranking.

Yet, incredibly, the first half of the championship game was scoreless. "I think we're in control of the game," Brown told his roommate, offensive guard John Wooten, during intermission. "Our defense is cracking, boom boom." Offensively, the Browns decided to open up more in the last half, running wider and throwing more. Their plans worked to perfection.

Early in the third period, Groza, the most production point-producer in NFL history, started the scoring with a 43-yard field goal. A few plays later, after Baltimore's second straight punt, Cleveland had possession again on its own 36. It was time, reasoned Ryan, to call "9-toss." He pitched out quickly to Brown, who swept around his own left end, took advantage of fine blocking and sprinted 46 yards to the Baltimore 18. On the next play, Ryan hit Collins in the end zone on a hook-and-go pass pattern, and the underdog Browns suddenly led, 10–0.

Ryan and Collins collaborated on two more touchdown strikes, Groza kicked two more conversions and another field goal, the Cleveland defense stifled Unitas all afternoon, and the Browns were truly the NFL champions, 27–0.

"We knew Baltimore had the best pass rush in the business," Ryan told writers in the dressing room afterward, "so our game plan was to keep Brown running and to pass strategically, with emphasis on the short stuff. As it turned out, we couldn't have figured it any better. The thing that surprised me was that they never adjusted to it, and if Jim weren't a human being, I would have run him on every play. That's how well it worked."

Jim had had a good, but by no means great, day (27 carries for 114 yards) on a day when Cleveland had had a handful of heroes, and for the first time in his professional career Jim was able to smile the smile of a league champion.

"We beat them hard, John," he told roommate Wooten, smiling.

"Attaway to go, Gary baby, really, baby," he told hero Collins, smiling.

"Yes, definitely," he told the steady stream of reporters who kept asking if this was his greatest thrill. Sometimes he said, "It's the biggest moment of my pro football career." Other times he said, "It's the biggest thrill of my career. I have had better days as an individual, but this is the most satisfying of all."

The nation's sportswriters and sportscasters obviously felt the same way about Jim's season. He had had better, but this was the most satisfying. Accordingly, a panel of 136 writers and announcers voted Jim Brown—over basketball's Bill Russell, baseball's Dean Chance, hockey's Bobby Hull, boxing's Cassius Clay, golf's Ken Venturi and auto racing's A. J. Foyt— the Professional Athlete of 1964.

CHAPTER 14

Perspective

SOMETIMES it seems that way, but Jim Brown actually does not do everything on the football field. He never plays defense, he rarely passes (only two completions in seven attempts in his eight professional seasons), and he seldom blocks.

But then again, Babe Ruth seldom stole bases.

No normal person, of course, expects Jim Brown to pass or to play defense. The only complaint comes when the subject of blocking is broached. Then the scattered few get going. They talk elaborately about how Marion Motley used to do it, or simply about how $60,000-a-year runner Jim Brown does not do it.

But seldom do they discuss logically. The fact is, even when he is not carrying the ball or running out for a pass, he is rarely called upon to block. When the Cleveland halfback carries, Jim's job is usually to act as a decoy. When the Cleveland quarterback passes,

150

Jim's job is usually to drift out and act as a tertiary receiver if the primary and secondary receivers are covered. Conceivably, Jim is called upon to block less than six times out of every hundred plays. Yet if the offensive play patterns demanded that he block much more, he most likely would be one of the best.

"He's simply an amazing athlete," says his present coach, Blanton Collier. "He'd be great at any position or in any sport. He could be the greatest defensive man, or the greatest blocker, in the history of the game if he wanted to be. But this would be a waste of talent. You could make a dray horse out of Man o' War, too."

In eight seasons, Brown has rushed for a record 10,768 yards and a record 89 touchdowns. Adding in the passes he has caught, he has scored 105 touchdowns. Only one other man in NFL history—Don Hutson, the great Green Bay end—has ever scored that many (105 in 11 seasons).

Yet with all his achievements, Jim has changed little in some ways. "In the last year, for the first time," says his high school coach, Ed Walsh, "I've heard him say '*my* blockers, *my* guards.' That isn't the slightest bit egotistical, but it's the only indication I've ever heard in my life that he is saying he has accomplished something."

In other ways he has changed tremendously. The boy who seldom spoke unless spoken to—and then not easily—has grown into an articulate man who has delivered speeches all around the country and who has branched into a broad range of communication media.

151

At one time or another in the last two or three years, he has written a weekly column in the Cleveland *Plain Dealer,* conducted his own shows on radio and television, and acted in the movies. All these extra efforts have earned quite a bit of extra money, but none has made him forget where it all began.

"He's come back six or seven times to speak in Manhasset," says his college benefactor, Ken Molloy, "and he won't accept even carfare on the Long Island Rail Road. He's even paid his own way from Cleveland."

With all his virtues (he does not smoke or drink, either), Jim does have at least one fault, as far as some sportswriters are concerned. He is not colorful copy. Unlike Babe Ruth, he is not boisterous. Unlike Ted Williams, he does not curse sportswriters. Unlike Jim Thorpe, he stays in shape.

Admittedly, though, these are minor failings. None of them will ever prevent people from praising Jim Brown as being just about everything from the greatest all-round athlete of all time to merely the greatest runner in football history.

Jim Brown's NFL Records

SCORING

Most Touchdowns, Lifetime

105	Jim Brown, Cleveland 1957–64	(89-r, 16-p)
105	Don Hutson, Green Bay 1935–45	(3-r, 101-p, 1-rb)
98	Lenny Moore, Balt. 1956–64	(52-r, 45-p, 1-rb)

Most Touchdowns, Season

20 Lenny Moore, Balt. 1964 (17-r, 3-p)
19 Jim Taylor, G. B. 1962 (19-r)
18 Steve Van Buren, Phil. 1945 (15-r, 2-p, 1-rb)
    Jim Brown, Clev. 1958 (17-r, 1-p)
    Jim Brown, Clev. 1962 (13-r, 5-p)

Most Touchdowns, Game

6 Ernie Nevers, Chi. Cards vs. Chi. Bears, Nov. 28, 1929 (6-r)
   Dub Jones, Clev. vs. Chi. Bears, Nov. 25, 1951 (4-r, 2-p)
5 Bob Shaw, Chi. Cards vs. Balt., Oct. 2, 1950 (5-p)
   Jim Brown, Clev. vs. Balt., Nov. 1, 1959 (5-r)
4 By many

RUSHING

Most Seasons Leading League

7 Jim Brown, Clev., 1957–61, 63–64
4 Steve Van Buren, Phil., 1945, 47–49
2 By five players

Most Consecutive Seasons Leading League

5 Jim Brown, Clev., 1957–61
3 Steve Van Buren, Phil., 1947—49
2 Bill Paschal, N.Y., 1943–44
   Joe Perry, S.F., 1953–54

ATTEMPTS

Most Attempts, Lifetime

2,070 Jim Brown, Clev., 1957–64
1,737 Joe Perry, S.F., 1950–60, 63; Balt., 1961–62
1,498 John Henry Johnson, S.F., 1954–56;
       Det., 1957–59: Pitt., 1960–64

Most Attempts, Season

305	Jim Brown, Clev.,	1961
291	Jim Brown, Clev.,	1963
290	Jim Brown, Clev.,	1959
280	Jim Brown, Clev.,	1964

Most Attempts, Game

38 Harry Newman, N.Y. vs. G.B., Nov. 11, 1934 (114 yards)
37 Jim Brown, Cleve. vs. Chi. Cards, Oct. 4, 1959 (147 yards)
35 George Grosvenor, Chi. Cards vs. G.B., Dec. 6, 1936 (100 yds.)
   Steve Van Buren, Phil. vs. N.Y. Bulldogs, Nov. 20, 1949 (174 yds.)

YARDAGE

Most Yards Gained, Lifetime

10,768 Jim Brown, Clev., 1957–64
 8,378 Joe Perry, S.F., 1950–60, 63; Balt., 1961–62
 6,768 Jim Taylor, G.B., 1958–64

Most Yards Gained, Season

1,863 Jim Brown, Clev., 1963
1,527 Jim Brown, Clev., 1958
1,474 Jim Taylor, G.B., 1962
1,446 Jim Brown, Clev., 1964
1,408 Jim Brown, Clev., 1961

Most Yards Gained, Game

237 Jim Brown, Clev. vs. L.A., Nov. 24, 1957 (31 attempts)
    Jim Brown, Clev. vs. Phil., Nov. 19, 1961 (34 attempts)
232 Bobby Mitchell, Clev. vs. Wash., Nov. 15, 1959 (21 attempts)
    Jim Brown, Clev. vs. Dallas, Sept. 22, 1963 (20 attempts)
223 Tom Wilson, L.A. vs. G.B., Dec. 16, 1956 (23 attempts)
    Jim Brown, Clev. vs. Phil., Nov. 3, 1963 (28 attempts)

AVERAGE GAIN

Highest Average Gain, Lifetime (700 att.)

5.20 Jim Brown, Clev., 1957–64 (2070-10,768)
4.83 Jim Taylor, G.B., 1958–64 (1400-6768)
4.82 Joe Perry, S.F., 1950–60, 63; Balt., 1961–62 (1737-8378)

Highest Average Gain, Season (100 att.)

9.9 Beattie Feathers, Chi. Bears, 1934 (101-1004)
6.8 Dan Towler, L.A., 1951 (126-854)
6.4 Jim Brown, Clev., 1963 (291-1863)

154

TOUCHDOWNS

Most Touchdowns, Lifetime

89   Jim Brown, Clev.,   1957–64
73   Jim Taylor, G.B.,   1958–64
69   Steve Van Buren, Phil.,   1944–51

Most Touchdowns, Season

19   Jim Taylor, G.B.,   1962
17   Jim Brown, Clev.,   1958
16   Lenny Moore, Balt.,   1964

Most Touchdowns, Game

6   Ernie Nevers, Chi. Cards vs. Chi. Bears,   Nov. 28, 1929
5   Jim Brown, Clev. vs. Balt.,   Nov 1, 1959
4   By many

Jim Brown

Season-by-Season

| Year | RUSHING | | | | RECEIVING | | | TOUCHDOWNS | |
	Att	Yds	Lg	Avg	Rec	Yds	Lg	R	P
1957	202	942	69	4.7	16	55	12	9	1
1958	257	1527	65	5.9	16	138	46	17	1
1959	290	1329	70	4.6	24	190	25	14	0
1960	215	1257	71	5.8	19	204	37	9	2
1961	305	1408	38	4.6	46	459	77	8	2
1962	230	996	31	4.3	47	517	53	13	5
1963	291	1863	80	6.4	24	268	83	12	3
1964	280	1446	71	5.2	36	340	40	7	2
Totals	2070	10768			228	2171		89	16

Att=Attempts
Yds=Yards gained
Lg=Longest gain
Avg=Average
Rec=Received
R=Running
P=Passing
(Statistics compiled by the NFL and Elias Sports Bureau.)

Index

Sport Shelf Books You Will Enjoy

Fran Tarkenton: The Scrambler
by Bill Libby

Bart Starr: The Cool Quarterback
by George Sullivan

The Glory Runners
by Al Hirshberg

Greatest Packers of Them All
by Chuck Johnson

Jim Brown: The Running Back
by Larry Klein

Joe Namath: A Football Legend
by David Lipman

The Johnny Unitas Story
by Lee Greene

The Pro Quarterbacks
by John Devaney

Pro Football's Unforgettable Games
by George Sullivan

Rockne of Notre Dame
by Delos W. Lovelace

The Author

LARRY KLEIN is the associate director of the National Collegiate Athletic Bureau. He has previously been assistant managing editor of *Sport* magazine and sports editor of *Newsweek* and over the years has written numerous articles for various sports magazines.

The author and his wife live in New York City.